Amos Bad Heart, an Oglala Sioux artist who as a child was present at the Little Bighorn battle, interprets the suicide death of Custer's last cavalryman. (Courtesy Professor Hubert Alexander)

KEEP THE LAST BULLET
FOR YOURSELF

General George Armstrong Custer. (Chicago Historical Society)

KEEP THE LAST
BULLET FOR
YOURSELF

**THE TRUE STORY OF
CUSTER'S LAST STAND**

Thomas B. Marquis

**THE TWO CONTINENTS PUBLISHING GROUP
A REFERENCE PUBLICATIONS BOOK**

Library of Congress Cataloging in Publication Data

Marquis, Thomas Bailey, 1869-1935.
  Keep the last bullet for yourself: the true story of
Custer's last stand.

  "A Reference Publications book."
  Bibliography: p.
  Includes index.
  1. Little Big Horn, Battle of the, 1876.   2. Custer, George Armstrong,
1839-1876.   I. Title.
E83.876.M282   1976   978.6′38   75-39093
ISBN 0-8467-0156-1

Production by Planned Production
Text design by Joyce C. Weston
Manufactured at Vail-Ballou Press, Inc., Binghamton, N.Y.
Printed in USA

Two Continents Publishing Group, Ltd.
30 East 42 Street
New York City 10017
and
Reference Publications, Inc.

CONTENTS

MAPS AND ILLUSTRATIONS

PREFACE

Few episodes in American history are more romantic or controversial than the Battle of the Little Bighorn. For a hundred years scholars have sought a satisfactory explanation of what occurred that fateful day in 1876 when Sioux and Cheyenne warriors overwhelmed the Seventh Cavalry, one of the most glamorous and efficient military units fielded by the United States. The impact on the American public at the loss of the colorful and flamboyant Custer brothers can be likened only to the recent and equally tragic Kennedy assassinations. "How could such a thing have occurred?" was the question on everyone's lips. The men with Custer were supposedly superior to their foes in every respect save numbers, yet the unorganized and poorly armed Indians inflicted one of the most stinging defeats ever imposed on the United States cavalry.

Of all the explanations put forward since then, none will be as controversial as the one offered here by Dr. Thomas B. Marquis, an obscure, dedicated physician who for many years in the first quarter of this century worked with the Cheyenne people on their Montana reservation located just a few miles from the Custer battlefield. A Custer buff, Marquis sought out and befriended the aged Sioux, Cheyenne, and Crow veterans of the Custer fight. Most of them did not speak English so he had to become adept at sign language to converse with them. No matter. Those old warriors liked the strange white man in his straw hat and celluloid collar who shared their hard existence. They spoke honestly and freely with him when most of them would have nothing to do with other whites.

After years of working with these veteran warriors and transcribing their stories, Marquis reached a simple but shocking conclusion about the Battle of the Little Bighorn: the troopers with Custer panicked and most of them committed suicide. Marquis knew his explanation would not be popular. It was so unpopular, in fact, he could not get it published even though he had written and published two other solid and worthwhile books on the subject: *Memoirs of a White Crow Indian* and *A Warrior Who Fought Custer.*

Marquis was bitterly disappointed. To him, *Memoirs of a White Crow Indian* and *A Warrior Who Fought Custer* had been merely a prelude to his analysis of the Custer battle. "Such a book has been my main objective ever since I first began studying the subject," he informed his daughters in March, 1934. "It was the main objective while I was gathering and writing the *White Crow* book and the *Warrior* book and all other writings of that general character. During all that time—and preceding—I was storing away notes, in classifications, for future use. Many of these notes are older than the first notes from *White Crow.*"

In another letter, written two months later, he admitted that several publishers had already rejected his Custer manuscript. No matter. "I have decided," he avowed, "to keep right on sending out and writing inquiries as to prospects, until some publisher accepted it and published it, or until old age and death overtakes me. It is *the one book* I have been preparing myself through ten or more years to write. The other writings have been side-channel studies." As he feared, death overtook him before he found a publisher.

After remaining unnoticed so long, this manuscript will now find a more receptive audience than it did a half century ago. Certainly this book deserves recognition whatever one chooses to believe about the battle. Marquis brought a scientific point of view to his historical research. He was a meticulous, careful scholar whose opinions should not be discarded out of hand. The suicide thesis will not be palatable but it must be considered.

This new contribution by Marquis to the Custer library offers more than fresh insights on the battle itself. Marquis also provides an outstanding description of Plains Indian warfare as well as an analysis of several important but less well known battles of the post-Civil War era when the northern Plains tribes lashed out in their last desperate attempt to keep the white man at bay.

The introduction by Joseph Medicine Crow, grandson of White Man Runs Him, one of General Custer's scouts, adds a further perspective. Joseph Medicine Crow, who is the official historian and anthropologist of the Crow tribe, knew Dr. Marquis personally, and is able to evaluate his work both from a contemporary standpoint as well as from that of tribal tradition.

HERMAN J. VIOLA

INTRODUCTION

". . . the most astounding military tragedy in the annals
of our western frontier warfare was caused by an unbridled
collapse of soldier morale resulting in a general self-extinction."

—*Thomas B. Marquis*

These are the hard-hitting opening words of a full length
manuscript by Dr. Marquis which have remained hidden somewhere in California for the last 42 years. The concluding sentence
of the same manuscript reads: "Maybe, after more than 200 years
of racial hatred, the Inexorable Law required General Custer
and his men to destroy themselves in vicarious blood expiation
to the Everywhere Spirit."

If the opening and closing sentences are any indication, this
latest addition to Custeriana promises to be controversial and perhaps shocking to some hard-core Custer fans. Unquestionably, this
book will refute the arguments and even destroy the credibility
of some well-known and widely accepted works. Also, it will support and strengthen the credibility of some works that have
hitherto had a poor reception, and which have even lacked ac-
ceptance all these years. At all events, it is time for another
"Custer" book. For some ten years there has been a noticeable

9

dearth of major new works on the Battle of Little Bighorn. There have, it is true, been some rehash versions, but nothing of major proportions, such as this work, has appeared. In my opinion, *Keep the Last Bullet For Yourself* qualifies as a highly original contribution based on first hand and on the spot research. It is, moreover, a work which cannot now possibly be duplicated, as the hand of time has removed from the scene those with whom Marquis talked and who had themselves lived through and participated in the extraordinary events of 1876.

I first met Thomas Bailey Marquis about 1926, when I was perhaps 12 years old. He came to my home to see my stepfather, John Whiteman Runs Him, wanting him to arrange an interview with my grandfather, White Man Runs Him, then the sole surviving member of General Custer's Crow scouts. The interview was arranged, and Marquis and my parents, John and Amy Whiteman (as they were known for short), became good friends. When my sister was born in 1929, Dr. Marquis named her after one of his daughters, Minnie Ellen (Hastings). My stepfather is now 83 years of age, and the last living son of any of the six Crow scouts of Custer. My mother Amy (Yellowtail) is about 79 years old.

Besides White Man Runs Him, Marquis interviewed nearly all the relatives and close associates of Custer's other Crow scouts (Curly, Goes Ahead, Hairy Moccasin, White Swan, Half Yellow Face). He obtained and recorded perhaps the best account of the special part these scouts played in the events of the Custer march from the Yellowstone to Medicine Tail Coulee, where Custer, the Son of Morning Star (as the scouts called him), eventually made his fatal contact with the "hostiles."

Dr. Marquis was proficient in the use of the Plains Indian sign language, a skill which helped him to gain the trust and friendship of the old Cheyenne and Crow warriors, which made him perhaps the first and only white man to whom they talked freely and with confidence. He also spoke in sign language with Thomas H. Leforge, a white man who was an adopted member of the Crow tribe, and who related his life story to Marquis, who had it published as *Memoirs of a White Crow Indian* (1929). Marquis and Leforge often rode about the reservation together in the doctor's old Model T Ford, with Marquis wearing a straw hat of the "eastern dude" variety, and a celluloid collar and bowtie, and Leforge wearing buckskins. On one occasion they became so engrossed in a lively sign language conversation, their arms flailing away, that they did not notice where they were going, and rammed another car. Leforge had formerly been a white

Crow scout, and, had he not broken his collar bone at that time, would doubtless have accompanied his friend and fellow scout Mitch Buoyer with Custer to the Little Bighorn Valley, never to return.

At first, when the doctor lived at Lame Deer, he would come to visit our home by driving over the winding dirt roads in his old Model T. Sometimes he would camp near the adjacent spring, living in his sheepherder's tent for several days at a time. Later, when he moved to Lodge Grass, we would often visit him. He was a vegetarian, and would serve my parents hot cocoa and dried bread, and would stay up late, as my mother recalls, playing checkers with my stepfather until the small hours.

Tempted as I am to review all the material in this book, I must nevertheless restrict my observations and remarks to some of those aspects that he touches upon which I consider uniquely revealing. I may give three examples.

First, Thomas Marquis' careful and detailed comparison of the respective mental attitudes and combat styles of the soldiers and of the warriors is an approach heretofore lightly treated or else ignored altogether, even although it gives a powerful answer to the question: Why did Custer lose? Second, Marquis' analysis of the battle based on comparisons with other battles between Indians and whites gives a clearer perspective to the Little Bighorn battle as a whole. Third, it is clear and obvious that Marquis launched his study with no axe to grind, no party to defend, and no preconceived theory to prove. Hence, he felt able courageously to discuss certain subjects generally shunted to one side by Custer students as too sensitive and controversial to be dealt with, such as, for example, the liquor question and the question of which side had superiority in arms.

The whiskey question has, indeed, long been a subject for controversy. Did General Custer and his men drink whiskey that fatal day of June 25, 1876? The question cannot be answered with a yes or a no, but rather with "yes and no"! Either answer can be supported with evidence, and advocates can either be academic or emotional in their positions.

Author Thomas Marquis was quite convinced that there was very little, if any, drinking on June 25. After detailed discussion of all probabilities, he concluded that "considering all known conditions, the explanation that whiskey vitally influenced the conduct of the soldiers that day has too thin a basis to be given serious credence." He pointed out that Custer himself did not drink, that Custer would not allow any drinking, especially by officers, and that the command started out from the Yellowstone quite "dry."

He also stated, however, that three days prior to Custer's departure from the Yellowstone there was considerable drinking, that Black Horse and some Cheyenne of Little Wolf's band found a tin cup containing whiskey at the last Custer camp on the Rosebud (on the evening of the 24th), and that Indians found whiskey in the canteens of some dead soldiers after the fight.

I shall not labor to advance my own opinions, but will merely repeat remarks and statements made by General Custer's Crow scouts. These men played a unique and important part in Custer's search for and pursuit of the "hostiles." They were almost constantly at his side, along with their interpreter and advisor, Mitch Buoyer, a half-Sioux married to a Crow woman. The General was quite considerate of them, and the scouts likewise thought kindly of him and regarded him with high esteem, as was symbolically shown by the name they gave him—Son of the Morning Star. But they felt very sorry for him when he made his decision to attack at once, heedless of their advice to wait for No Hip Bone (General Gibbon, so-called because he limped from a Civil War wound) and The Other One (General Terry). As his last act of consideration to his faithful scouts, General Custer dismissed them just prior to his final charge down Medicine Tail Coulee.

But, as regards the whiskey question, all of the Crow scouts stated, at one time or another, that there was indeed whiskey drinking on June 25, the day of Custer's attack. These men were all loyal to and had a high regard for the General, and would have no reason or ulterior motive to discredit him in any way. Pretty Shield, the widow of Goes Ahead, stated to her biographer, Frank B. Linderman (*Pretty Shield: Medicine Woman of the Crows,* 1972 reproduction):

> My man, Goes Ahead, Hairy Moccasin, and White Man Runs Him, knew that there were more Lacota and Cheyenne somewhere ahead than there were bullets in the belts of the blue soldiers who were with Son-of-the-Morning-Star. They believed that they ought to tell him this, so they went back and told him. But he only said "Go on again," and then drank from a straw-covered bottle.

Pretty Shield concluded her remarks about the drinking by saying to Mr. Linderman: "Sign-Talker, too much drinking may have made that great soldier-chief foolish on that day when he died."

George Curly, aged about 61 or 62, grandson of Curly the scout, related on November 10, 1975.

> I recall my grandfather often telling that during the march up the Rosebud he was dispatched with a message to the rear of the column. As he approached the main supply mules he noticed a smaller outfit some distance back so he went there instead. Here some soldiers were drinking whiskey from a keg and he noticed that the mules carried a small keg on each side. Then again, after the first sighting of the enemy camp and prior to the attack, the march down Dense Ashwood Creek (Reno Creek) was halted. These same mules were brought up and the kegs were opened and whiskey poured into the cups of the soldiers. We scouts joined the line and drank the "bad water."

Robert Yellowtail, aged 87, once a son-in-law of White Man Runs Him, often repeated the old scout's version of the drinking halt as follows:

> While coming down Dense Ashwood Creek with the General and us scouts with Mitch Buoyer at the head of the column, Son of the Morning Star signalled a halt. While we were munching on hard-tacks and bacon, pack mules were brought up quickly, each carrying small kegs, one on each side. These were unplugged and soldiers filed by with their cups to receive their share. We scouts joined in; before long my finger tips and lips tingled and felt numb. Our interpreter, Mitch Buoyer, explained that the whiskey was to make the soldiers brave.

It was my personal observation on several occasions that White Man Runs Him would become irritated or disgusted with interviewers who showed disinterest or incredulity when he mentioned the drinking incident. The same disinterest or incredulity was a reaction also shown by such interviewers to the other scouts, and some indicated that they were admonished by "influential people" to desist from saying that there was drinking by the soldiers. George Curly went on to say that his grandfather recalled that when the Crow scouts sighted the Sioux camp, and one went back to tell the General, "he soon came galloping madly up the high hill and after peering through his 'glasses' he dashed down the hill like a drunk man." Then later, as Custer veered off north from Reno's column, "he was already quite inebriated." This, coming from Curly, regarded as General Custer's favorite scout, poses a serious accusation, to say the least.

It is now a hundred years since the Battle of the Little Bighorn, a respectable length of time which perhaps at last gives us the right to make some observations and conclusions based upon hindsight.

Custer's Seventh Cavalry alone could have inflicted a serious, if not a devastating, defeat upon the "hostile" Sioux and Cheyenne that day in June 1876 along the banks of the Little Bighorn River.

But why did they not do so? Because General Custer, his officers, and his men did not know that day: (1) That the Indians were caught off guard and were unprepared for instant counter-attack; (2) That the attack on the camp from two sides and the ensuing panic of women, children, old people, and horses not only physically hindered the warriors, but also laid a psychological burden upon them; (3) That the Plains Indians' style of fighting did not lend itself to orderly and unified action, but that each warrior performed as an individual, motivated mainly by the desire to count coup (merely touch a live enemy) out of heroics, rather than to kill for the sake of killing; (4) That the Seventh Cavalry had at their disposal weapons and fire-power vastly superior to the few rifles, including old Civil War muzzle-loaders, that the Indians had available.

On the other hand, the Indians—head chiefs, war chiefs, and warriors—for their part did not know the following: (1) That many of the soldiers were raw recruits with no previous battle experience; (2) That the average soldier was under the impression that the Indians' primary purpose was to capture whites for the purpose of inflicting fiendish tortures upon them, and was therefore suicide prone; (3) That at least the soldiers under the immediate command of Custer may have been given whiskey which impaired their judgment and performance.

Thomas B. Marquis was born in Oceola, Missouri, on December 19, 1869. His on-the-scene study of the Battle of Little Bighorn had covered about ten years when an untimely heart attack ended his work on March 22, 1935. He was in his sixty-sixth year. During this time he had, as I mentioned earlier, interviewed Indian survivors of the battle and the relatives of other participants, as well as some white soldiers and scouts who had participated in the 1876 campaign against the Sioux and Cheyenne. While he wrote two other books, and numerous pamphlets and magazine articles directly or indirectly related to the battle, others must often have wondered, as I did myself, why he did not write his own complete account and analysis of the Little Bighorn conflict. We did not know that he had in fact done so. He left behind a complete manuscript which has been ready for the press at any time during the last 40 years.

Could it be, may I add, that that same Everywhere Spirit that he himself speaks of had "arranged" for the long-hidden manuscript to come alive as a book during the Centennial Year of the Battle of Little Bighorn in particular, and the Bicentennial Year of the country in general? As the news of Custer's disaster saddened the gala centennial celebration in Philadelphia, so perhaps this new book about the famed battle of 1876 will cast a pall of thought over the gala atmosphere that marks the celebration of its centennial.

JOSEPH MEDICINE CROW

Lodge Grass
Montana
January, 1976

AUTHOR'S STATEMENT

Custer's last battle has been cherished in our national lore as a resolute and glorious death-struggle. But, on the contrary, it was a pitiable fiasco. The soldiers weakened and swept themselves to destruction.

This adverse judgment has plenty of evidence to support it. The purpose of this book is to present that evidence. The intention is to prove that the most astounding military tragedy in the annals of our western frontier warfare was caused by an unbridled collapse of soldier morale resulting in a general self-extinction.

THOMAS B. MARQUIS

THE BACKGROUND

As the white man moved westward across North America in the 19th century, he took possession, step by step, of lands that had once belonged to the Indians.

In the 1870s, rumors spread that there was gold to be had in the Black Hills of South Dakota, a region sacred to the Sioux, and which had been guaranteed to them in perpetuity by the United States government by the Treaty of 1868. In 1874, in violation of the treaty, but with permission from Washington though not from the Sioux, General George Armstrong Custer led a force of Seventh Cavalrymen into the area. The troops were protecting a scientific expedition which included geologists, who ascertained that there was indeed gold in the Hills.

By 1875, word of the discovery had spread, and a white gold rush towards the Hills began. The United States Army, after some attempts to maintain the Treaty by keeping the prospectors out, gave up trying. Conflicts between whites and Indians broke out, leading to retaliations. The United States government of the day, unable and perhaps unwilling to control the gold-hungry whites, attempted to buy the Black Hills from the Sioux, but found them unprepared to sell. The Indians, outraged, became increasingly hostile to and distrustful of the whites. Numbers of Indians, alienated by white ways, retired to the unceded lands further west, in Montana Territory and the Wyoming area, the last great hunting grounds in the Yellowstone River region and around the Bighorn Mountains. Here, away from the reservations and the watchful observation of the government's agents, warrior bands attempted to continue their old and free life style, away from white constraints.

The United States government, disturbed by the Indian-white conflicts which had occurred, subjected to the pressure of anti-Indian sentiment, and doubtless wishing to extend its authority another stage, notified the Indians through whatever channels were available to them that all Indians who did not come into the reservations by January 31, 1876, would be classified as "hostile," and turned over to the United States Army for appropriate action. The Indians living in the unceded territories—mostly Northern Cheyenne and Sioux—ignored the demand. Thus began the Sioux War of 1876-77.

To subdue the "hostiles," the United States Army, in the spring of 1876, sent out three separate columns under the overall command of General Alfred H. Terry. These columns were to converge in the heart of the hunting, or unceded, territory near the mouth of the Little Bighorn River. One column, led by General John Gibbon, was to march down southeastward from Montana Territory. Another, under General George Crook, was to march northwestward from Fort Fetterman in Wyoming. A third, the "Dakota column," technically headed by Terry, but in fact under the command of Custer, was to march southwestward from Fort Abraham Lincoln in North Dakota.

The problem was expected to be to find the Indians and to engage them in combat. Custer, it was confidently anticipated, would bear the brunt of any combat that might occur, since he had experience in Indian fighting. A newspaper correspondent accompanied him, possibly to send news of a victory against the Indians back east in time for the national centennial being celebrated in Philadelphia that summer. Such a victory would have advanced Custer's career, overshadowing some recent difficulties he had been having with his superiors in Washington, and perhaps opening up political possibilities for a Democrat who was already a dashing if controversial national figure.

Custer finally caught up with the Indians on June 25, 1876. But instead of winning a victory, he and all his troops, except those he had despatched on other missions, were annihilated together at the Battle of Little Bighorn. Even the newspaper correspondent did not live to report the defeat.

CUSTER HIMSELF

George Armstrong Custer was born on December 5, 1839, at New Rumley, Ohio. During his early boyhood, his family moved to Monroe, Michigan, where he grew up. During his growing years, reports show him as a youth full of romping liveliness but without any viciousness in his make-up. The Custer family were not people of importance, politically, socially, or otherwise, but all of them were of sound and respectable character.

Custer's first step into public life came when he was accepted as a student at West Point. His career there has been represented as somewhat tarnished by acts of disobedience. But writers have sometimes pointed with pride to evidence of unruly conduct at school by men who later became heroes. Such representations are often exaggerated, and sometimes are even invented in order to create reader interest. Custer's subsequent career indicates that he probably was an unusually fiery military cadet. But it also indicates that he must have done much studying and that, on the whole, he was more a source of satisfaction to his instructors than a troublemaker.

He graduated from West Point in June 1861. The Civil War was beginning, and young officers were needed. His first duty assignment was as a lieutenant in Company G of the Second Cavalry. Major Innes Palmer was in command of the regiment, which formed part of the armed forces under the command of General Irvin McDowell. It was not long before Custer's superiors noted that he was particularly talented. He was promoted in rank, being placed on General George B. McClellan's staff as an aide-de-camp. His conduct in advanced positions brought him to special notice, and promotions came again and again. On June 29, 1863, within two years of his first appointment, he was made a brigadier general of volunteers, leading all of the Michigan cavalry forces engaged in the war. In October 1864 he was brevetted as a major general of volunteers. In April 1865, during the last few days of the war, he distinguished himself in cavalry operations against General Robert E. Lee. He was present when the great Confederate leader surrendered to General Grant at Appomattox, Virginia.

After the Civil War, Custer was sent to Texas, to stamp out the lingering rebellion in that state. He was in command of 13 regiments of infantry and about the same number of cavalry regiments. These forces were scattered here and there over the state. There was little fighting, for most of the last-ditch Confederate leaders had fled into Mexico. Custer's troops served primarily to demonstrate their military strength and to discourage any further resistance to the authority of the United States government.

At about this time, General Grant recommended Custer to Emperor Maximilian, who was then ruling Mexico. Maximilian offered Custer an appointment as adjutant general of the Mexican army. The salary offered was $16,000 per year—exactly double the pay he was receiving as major general. Custer applied to his own military superiors for a leave of absence of one year, in order that he might accept the appointment. But the leave of absence was denied, and Custer stayed in the United States.

In February 1864, while he was brigadier general commanding the Michigan cavalry with the Army of the Potomac, he made a brief visit to his family in Monroe, Michigan. During this visit he married Elizabeth Bacon. After the wedding, his bride accompanied him on his return to the Virginia battle area. There she remained, moving from place to place in order to keep near him throughout the remainder of the war. She later went with him to Texas, to Fort Riley in Kansas, and to other places that he established as his central bases during his subsequent campaigns. The Custers had no children. Elizabeth Custer survived her husband for almost 57 years. She died on April 4, 1933, aged 91.

During the Civil War, Custer held his high rankings in his

capacity as an officer commanding volunteer soldiers. When the volunteer armies were disbanded, many regular army officers who had been holding high commissions were downgraded in rank in order to take their places in a regular army that was much constricted in size. Custer himself was reduced in rank to captain, although in July 1866 he was promoted to lieutenant colonel. His pay was only $2,000 a year, as compared to the $8,000 he had earned as a major general, or the $16,000 he had been offered by Maximilian.

Other officers prominent in the 1876 campaign who had also been demoted in rank after the Civil War were Alfred A. Terry, George A. Crook, and John A. Gibbon. Terry and Crook, who had both been major generals, were brigadier generals in 1876. Gibbon, who had been a brigadier general, was downgraded to colonel, although throughout the military operations of 1876 he commanded four troops of the Second Cavalry as well as seven companies of his own infantrymen. By custom, the highest military title any particular officer had ever held continued to be employed as a courtesy title in everyday life. Thus, although Gibbon held the rank of colonel in 1876, and Custer that of lieutenant colonel, the title of general was still applied to each of them, except in the army's official or documentary transactions.

Much may be learned from Mrs. Custer's books about her husband's personality, although some allowance must be made for the probability that she was biased in some of her estimates of him. She records his height as six feet and his weight as 170 pounds. He had blue-gray eyes and was sandy complexioned. His hair was auburn with a tinge of red. When he went unshaven, as happened when he went campaigning on the Plains, his beard was also auburn or reddish colored. His frame was all bone and muscle, and he was physically strong in proportion to his size. He was intensely energetic and seemed never to be idle. Everything he did was done vigorously, and even strenuously.

His superabundance of spirit was evident in the wild demonstrations of joy he exhibited whenever something happened that especially pleased him. Mrs. Custer tells of his boyish rompings in their home quarters on such occasions. He would playfully smash up the furniture and toss his wife into the air, while emitting tremendous and characteristic whoops of glee. Mirth, hilarity, and practical joking were dominant traits. He was obliged to exert considerable will power to hold his liveliness within proper bounds at times when the occasion required it.

Mrs. Custer writes of her husband as talking rapidly, even incoherently, when he got warmed up in his efforts to express himself. At such times he stammered, stuttered, and almost sputtered. This form of mental agitation was evident in the attempts at public speaking that he made while on leave of absence in some of the eastern cities. The same trait was also to be found in his father. The elder Custer had a reputation as an excitable and partisan argufier, especially when politics were discussed.

Custer's own book, *My Life on the Plains,* published early in 1876, reveals him as a sarcastic person who ridiculed those people and things not in conformity with his ideas. The common talk among those soldiers who knew him was that he was not popular with either his men or his officers. He was too cutting, too sarcastic. His subordinates lived in constant dread of being the target of one of his biting remarks, or of receiving one of his rasping orders to perform some unusually harsh duty. Alexander Burkman, who was Custer's orderly for several years, and who lived on for another 50 years after his death, told of his having a naturally hot temper. But while Custer was often explosive, he also often made amends by making a prompt apology or conferring a favor. Such behavior seems consistent with what we know of his character. Malice aforethought was alien to him, nor was he one to hatch schemes against others. All the authentic reports that we have indicate this, as do his own writings. All indications are also that his belittling of other people was always in a semimirthful vein, and that he never resorted to vilification or abuse.

He loved horses and dogs and made pets of as many of them as he could. He also had other pets—a wildcat, a prairie dog, a porcupine, a raccoon, a badger, and a wild turkey are all mentioned in his wife's writings. She also tells of a field mouse he captured and tamed. He kept it in an empty ink bottle on his desk. He took it out at times, taught it some tricks, and played with it. Because of his wife's horror of mice, however, he reluctantly released it outside. But it kept coming back and trying to resume an association it had evidently enjoyed.

When he went to Fort Riley in October 1866 as lieutenant colonel of the embryo Seventh Cavalry, he took four horses and ten dogs with him. Most of the dogs were deer hounds. In his writings he tells of watching his dogs chase antelope during his campaign journey through western Kansas and its contiguous territory in the summer of 1867. He wrote that "the antelope were in no danger of being caught by the dogs." They also chased buffalo, harassed them, but brought none of them down. He again went hunting with his dogs in 1868, 1869, 1873, and doubtless in other years. On one occasion in 1868, however, the dogs proved a hindrance to him. He and his men were stealing upon an Indian camp. But the Custer dogs began to fight, either among themselves or with the Indian dogs. The Indians were warned, and all of them escaped.

Custer had a variety of firearms, some of them relics, in his personal collection. He was an enthusiastic hunter. In a letter written to his wife when he was on the Yellowstone River in 1873, he tells of using his new Springfield rifle to kill 41 antelope, 4 buffalo, 4 elk, 7 deer, 2 wolves, 1 red fox, and large numbers of geese, ducks, prairie chickens, and sage hens.

His book tells of the first buffalo he ever saw. He and his cavalry were out on their first military expedition, traveling northward from Fort Larned, Kansas, in 1867. Custer and his bugler were far forward and to one side of the cavalry when they saw a lone buffalo bull. They put their horses into a run towards the buffalo. Custer's mount outran the ordinary cavalry plug, so that the commander soon found himself alone in the pursuit. He had a whoopingly joyful time for several miles, with his swift thoroughbred racing just behind or at the side of the big Plains animal. Finally he decided to shoot. He drew his revolver and aimed it. Just then his horse made a sudden jerking swerve. The trigger was pulled accidentally. The bullet crashed straight into the brain of the horse, and it fell dead.

Custer had a personal library that was rather extensive for the times as well as for the conditions under which he lived. According to his wife's account, he was greedy for books, especially instructive ones. This testimony tends to be borne out by his own accomplishments in writing. The fact that he had a creditable collection of books at his home at Fort Abraham Lincoln, near the site of present-day Bismarck, North Dakota, was vouched for by Mrs. J. E. Chappell, long a resident of Buffalo, Wyoming. As a girl she was for a time at Fort Abraham Lincoln, where her father was an officer. Among the books she herself borrowed from Custer's home library were Prescott's *Conquest of Mexico* and *Conquest of Peru*, Bayard Taylor's travel stories, and various other books of a similar kind.

Custer wrote a number of articles which were published in the *Galaxy Magazine*, owned by Sheldon & Co. of New York. The same firm later published them in book form, under the title *My Life on the Plains*. The articles covered his experiences on the southern Plains in 1867-69. The book had 256 pages, printed in small type. The small type and the full pages make the contents about double that of the average novel. He was aged 28 to 30 when he had the experiences which form the basis of the book, and the writing of it was done when he was 33 to 36. The book has merit, but it also has a great many more words than necessary. The narrative and the descriptions are ornamented with verbal curlicues and flourishings. Although an editor's pencil would have improved it, surely it then would not have depicted so well the natural Custer. As published, the book sparkles. All of it is interesting, and much of it is intensely interesting.

He worked on his *Galaxy* articles while campaigning no less than when he was at home. An 1873 letter sent from the Yellowstone to his wife tells her that he had written a long article for the magazine during a two-day stop at a certain camp. In a letter dated June 17, 1876, written nine days before he was killed, he tells his wife of having mailed a *Galaxy* article that day, to go in the steamboat mail from the mouth of the Tongue River.

His campaign letters to his wife, as published in 1885 in the appendix to her *Boots and Saddles*, exemplify his literary style, although she mentions that they have been cut down for publication. That he wrote profusely is evident. In one of his letters he mentions that it consists of 32 pages despite his efforts to "boil it down," as he said the *Galaxy* people were urging him to do in his writings.

He was on close friendly terms with Lawrence Barrett, the great stage tragedian, whom he saw on his visits to New York. Perhaps it was this association that imbued Custer with thoughts of taking theatrical lessons. In one of his 1873 letters to his wife he expresses the wish that they could get a competent instructor in private theatricals for the next winter season at the post. Another letter expressed a longing to take music lessons. His wife writes that he had a good ear for music, and she cites evidence to prove it. As a taxidermist he acquired a proficiency satisfying to himself. It is reasonable to believe that he may have had other accomplishments.

The long hair that Custer allowed to grow for several years may be thought of as an affectation or as a sign of a wish to attract attention. But long hair was not unusual among the Civil War men, and was quite the common style among plainsmen when Custer went into service in the Indian country. It appears that he did in fact enjoy the public attention he attracted, although it does not appear that his long hair had much to do with putting him in the public eye. At all events, he adopted the short hair fashion during the year preceding his death. Frederick A. Bond, a veteran of the Seventeenth Infantry who served at Fort Abraham Lincoln or in that vicinity, and who later published his recollections of Custer during the six months before the 1876 campaign, says that Custer's hair was clipped close to his head during all of that time. Sergeant John Martin, trumpeter for the Seventh Cavalry in 1876, wrote in the *Cavalry Journal* for July 1923 about Custer on the day he was killed. Martin said Custer had "hair cut short—not very short, but not long as he had worn it in previous times." In addition, Mrs. Custer repeatedly stated that he had been wearing his hair short for some time before the 1876 campaign. It is likely that both his hair and his beard were rather shaggy when he was killed, as he had been about six weeks away from the post. It was the standard custom among cavalrymen to let their hair and beards grow when they went campaigning.

Custer's habitual style of dress was vivid. Some explanation of it was given by Mrs. Custer in a writing she sent to the Bighorn County Library in Hardin, Montana, to accompany an enlarged reproduction of a Civil War photograph of Custer by the renowned Mathew Brady. Mrs. Custer wrote:

> The wide felt hat was captured from a Confederate. The shirt, of blue flannel, was purchased from a government gunboat in the Potomac River. The necktie was scarlet. General Custer began to wear the red tie when he was made a brigadier general and assigned to the command of the Michigan cavalry brigade. The entire brigade adopted the tie, and when the General was appointed major general and given command of the Third Cavalry division of the Army of the Potomac, they also wore them. The badge on the tie was that of the Michigan brigade, with the motto of the state and the name of Custer.

In her book Mrs. Custer relates that at Fort Abraham Lincoln she planned a pleasant surprise for her husband by making him some red flannel shirts. When she presented them, Custer broke into a succession of his stentorian whoops. He called Captain Tom Custer, his brother, who joined him in ridiculing her ideas about the color a soldier should wear, since red would make him an easy target for a bullet. They invited others to join the joke on her. Custer declared he was going to wear the shirts in deference to her evident wish that he be shot. But she prevented his doing so by slyly giving them as a present to Burkman, Custer's orderly.

This action brought forth renewed teasing. Her husband and his friends pretended to believe that, having learned of the bullet-attracting power of red clothing, she adopted this means for getting rid of Burkman.

Sergeant Martin's *Cavalry Journal* article says that at the time of the Little Bighorn battle Custer was wearing a blue-gray flannel shirt, buckskin trousers, long boots, and a company hat. At the Reno court-martial trial, Lieutenant Charles C. DeRudio said that both Custer and Lieutenant William W. Cooke, his adjutant, were wearing blue shirts and buckskin trousers. DeRudio also told of Captain Tom Custer wearing a full suit of buckskin.

In addition to the Brady photograph, Mrs. Custer also sent a fine buckskin suit, often worn by her husband on his campaigns, to the Bighorn County Library. Visitors to the Library often thought that this was the suit worn by Custer when he was killed. They were wrong. All of the clothing he was wearing then, as well as all of the clothing worn by every one of his men killed, was taken by the Indians.

On two occasions Custer was penalized for military offenses. The first occasion was just after he returned to Fort Riley after his summer campaign of 1867. During the campaign, in the course of which he had tried to catch Indians on the plains of western Kansas, he had had much trouble with soldiers deserting or attempting to desert. In one instance the deserters were fired upon, and one of them was killed before the others were recaptured. During the return march, after Fort Wallace was reached by the main column, Custer and a few chosen companions cut loose and went on ahead to the home post, arriving there some days before the rest.

Custer's own book tells of these incidents, and it also tells of his being released for about a year in discredit. It does not, however, reveal the specific charges against him. P. E. Byrne, in his *Soldiers of the Plains* (1926), discusses the case. He says that Custer was arrested and tried by court-martial proceedings on charges of shooting deserters without trial and of leaving his command without an authoritative order to do so. For these offenses he was suspended from rank and command for one year, and he forfeited one year's pay.

The second occasion that Custer came into conflict with military law was early in 1876. The grounds of the threats held over him for several weeks at that time have never been publicly clarified. It appears, however, that something in his conduct brought him into discord with William W. Belknap, then Secretary of War in President Grant's cabinet. Belknap was being crowded by a congressional investigating committee, probing charges of corruption in the placing of sutlers at military posts and—in collusion with corrupt Indian agents—in the management of Indian affairs. Custer was summoned to Washington to give testimony before the committee. His testimony was, however, rather tame in comparison with the previous utterances he had been making. Although Belknap resigned before the charges against him were fully disposed of, Custer was generally discredited as having made statements informally that he was not willing or not able to substantiate under oath.

It is not improbable that Custer's ineffectiveness as a witness was because he was threatened with a court-martial himself if he should give testimony fatal to Belknap. Some of his fervent declarations had offended President Grant, who was a strong friend of Belknap, his Secretary of War. There were good grounds, in Custer's *Galaxy Magazine* articles, for a court-martial trial and conviction, regardless of the outcome of the Belknap case. In particular, his writings mercilessly ridiculed the ways of General Alfred Sully in handling the Seventh Cavalry during the enforced absence of Custer in the summer of 1868. These writings, which also form part of his book, certainly show that Custer forgot proper military decorum in making public disparaging thoughts concerning an officer who was superior in rank to himself and who had also supplanted him in his command.

Custer remained in suspense in Washington while his regiment was making ready to go on the 1876 expedition. Then, on his way to his home post, he stopped for a time in Chicago, headquarters of General Philip Henry Sheridan. Finally, at the urgent request of Sheridan and General Terry, commander of his department, Custer was allowed to rejoin his regiment and lead it in the campaign. It has been represented that he pleaded in a pitiable way with Sheridan and Terry in order to enlist their support. It seems more probable that he made plain to them his real case, and that he did in fact know much more than he told the congressional committee. He may also have made it plain to them that court-martial proceedings against him might disclose political corruption in a way very embarrassing to the administration, and that his detractors knew this, so that he had no fear of being court-martialed.

It would seem a rational supposition that Indian agents and whiskey traders of those times were hostile to Custer and were doing whatever they could to put him down. Certainly he gave them grounds for wishing him ill. Throughout the years of his service on the western Plains, he, like other army officers of all ranks, was constantly advocating that civilian officials be entirely eliminated from the conduct of Indian affairs, and that all the Indians be placed under control of the War Department. His writings contain heavy criticism of the civilian management of the Indians. The civilians concerned countered with charges of ruthlessness by army officers in general in administering Indian affairs. They regarded Custer as among the most ruthless of them all.

The belief that Custer's actions in the 1876 military campaign were especially influenced by his fear of an impending court-martial is contradicted not only by his original ground for feeling secure but also by other circumstances. Up to the last day or two of his life, in which other matters came up to puzzle him, his conduct was the exact opposite of what might have been expected from a man worried by thoughts of court-martial, or indeed by anything else. He was his usual abundantly animated, industrious, and tireless self—throwing clods at his sleeping younger brother, Boston, to startle him into thoughts of a night attack by Indians; playing practical jokes on his other brother, Captain Tom; and accepting with uproarious mirth whatever jokes his immediate associates played upon him. Furthermore, during that time he also wrote and mailed another *Galaxy* article.

It appears he was a total abstainer from alcohol. Mrs. Custer writes that he never drank liquor, and that they never kept any on hand for medicine. It might be thought that she overstated his virtue in this regard, but there is ample proof to sustain her declaration. Custer often expressed his disapproval of liquor. In 1873, while he was on the Yellowstone expedition, he confiscated and spilled out several barrels of trader whiskey that had been brought into the vicinity of his soldiers, even although this action brought him a reprimand from a superior officer.

A letter from General Edward S. Godfrey to the author may be considered as strong testimony concerning Custer's personal habits. Godfrey was one of the officers with the Seventh Cavalry from the time of its birth, so it may be presumed he was well acquainted with its leader. In this letter, written on September 11, 1928, when he was 84, Godfrey wrote:

> I never saw or heard of his taking a drink of alcoholic liquor while in the Seventh Cavalry. I never heard, or heard of, him using profane or unchaste language, or telling an

unchaste story. He did love to gamble—not for the money, but for the thrill of the game. During his later years he did not put up stakes, but, watching a game, would often take some man's place and play his hand.

Despite his reputation for ruthlessness, Custer expressed a misgiving concerning the methods of waging war against the Indians on at least one occasion. In one of his narratives he describes how, during the night, he placed his forces round a Cheyenne camp ready for a surprise attack at dawn. Various sounds were heard and investigated. All proved to be of no special significance. Then:

> I turned to retrace my steps when another sound was borne to my ear through the cold, clear atmosphere of the valley. It was the distant cry of an infant; and, savages though they were, and justly outlawed by the number and atrocity of their recent murders and depredations on the helpless settlers of the frontier, I could not but regret that in a war such as we were forced to engage in, the mode and circumstances of battle would prevent possible discrimination.

Impetuous courage may be regarded as Custer's paramount character trait. It may be considered that it was this trait, insufficiently checked by considerations of either prudence or civility, and associated with exhibitionistic overtones, that led him headlong into indiscretions that caused resentment. This resentment, harbored by the victims of his witticisms, greatly augmented the flood of posthumous blame poured on him after the disaster at Little Bighorn, when he was accused of unwarrantedly plunging ahead. It is the opinion of the author, after a long and disinterested analysis of the circumstances attending his last battle, that none of Custer's conduct at that time affords a proper ground for the intemperate accusations subsequently brought against him. The real foundation for the adverse criticisms leveled at him originates in those many occasions when, heedless of his own interests and often of the justifiable interests of others, Custer, in his caustic manner, rubbed fur the wrong way.

CUSTER'S SEVENTH CAVALRY

The Seventh Cavalry was founded in July 1866. Colonel Andrew J. Smith was assigned as its commanding officer, and its assembling headquarters was at Fort Riley, Kansas. Custer, who previously held the rank of captain, was promoted to lieutenant colonel, and he joined the regiment in October. Subordinate officers were also assigned, and men were enlisted or transferred from other army units. Some training took place during the winter months. By the time spring came, the Seventh Cavalry had the semblance of a genuine regiment.

The first field movement of this new branch of the United States Regular Army began in April 1867. Colonel Smith was on detached duty elsewhere, so Lieutenant Colonel Custer held the active command. In fact, it appears that the original plan was to let Custer undertake the active leadership of the regiment. Neither Colonel Smith nor Colonel Samuel D. Sturgis, who succeeded him in May 1869, ever led the Seventh Cavalry in any campaign until after Custer's death. It was not until 1877 that Sturgis went into the field, in pursuit of the Nez Percé Indians in Montana.

The first expedition in 1867 was undertaken for the purpose of clearing the central and southern parts of the western Plains of those Indians who had been harassing white settlers and trav-

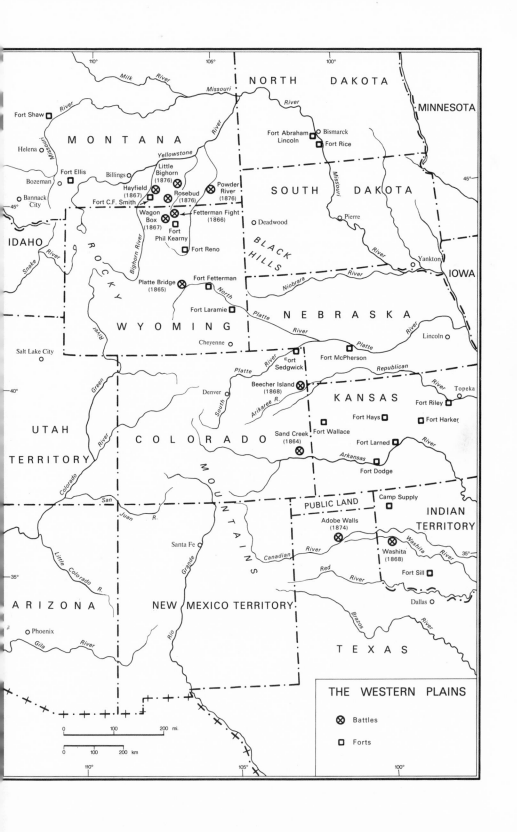

elers. General Winfield Scott Hancock came from department
headquarters in St. Louis to launch the expedition. At Fort
Leavenworth, Kansas, he took command of six companies of
infantry and a battery of artillery, bringing them on to Fort
Riley. Here he annexed to his command another company of infantry and four troops of the Second Cavalry. According to
Custer's book: "It was at this point that I joined the expedition."

The regiment marched to Fort Harker, Kansas, where, as the
Custer book relates, "our force was strengthened by the addition
of two more troops of cavalry." The regimental affiliation of
these two troops is not specified. The march was then resumed,
with Fort Larned as the destination. Indian agents had been arranging with various tribes for a great peace council to be held
at Fort Larned on April 10. The soldiers arrived there on April 7.
Two days later a big snow storm occurred, and this, together
with some delays on the part of the Indians, resulted in the
soldiers remaining encamped at Fort Larned for several days.
The regiment then marched northwest from Larned up Walnut
Creek, towards a place where a large number of Cheyenne and
some Sioux were encamped.

The march was halted from time to time, whenever Indian
delegations promised a council, and was then resumed when the
promises were not fulfilled. The chiefs with whom they dealt
that are mentioned in Custer's book include Tall Bear, Gray
Beard, Medicine Wolf, and Roman Nose, all of whom were
Cheyenne, and Pawnee Killer, who was a Sioux. Earlier, Hancock had brought with him two Cheyenne children, a boy and
a girl, who had been captured at the time of Colonel John M.
Chivington's attack on a Cheyenne camp at Sand Creek in south-
eastern Colorado in 1864. The children had been well cared for
by white families, but the Indians had learned about them and
wanted them back. At the earlier council at Fort Larned they
had been handed back to their own people.

Concluding that the Indians were tricking him into delays that
might help him in some way, Hancock decided to capture the
whole body of them in the Cheyenne camp. Custer and his cavalrymen were ordered to surround the camp during the night,
and they did so. The infantry and artillery were held in readiness.
At daylight the next morning, the entire camp was still there. But
all of the Indians who had been in it were gone.

"It was then decided," Custer later wrote, "that with eight
troops of cavalry I should start in pursuit of the Indians at early
dawn on the following morning, April 15." Earlier he had made

mention of four troops of the Second Cavalry leaving Fort Riley, and of two additional troops, regiment unspecified, being at Fort Harker. The reference to eight troops going on the pursuit expedition shows that somewhere two more troops had been added. It is presumable, however, that all the eight troops may have belonged to the Seventh Cavalry.

The trail led them northward. About 15 miles from Fort Hays, Kansas, they found that the Indians had burned a stage station and killed all the employees. On May 3 the cavalrymen reached Fort Hays without having caught up with the Indians. Here they went into camp to await supplies which they had expected but which had not yet arrived. Hancock, leading the infantry and artillery contingents, arrived a few days after Custer had gone into camp. He then went back to Fort Leavenworth to urge the forwarding of the supplies. When the supplies finally arrived, Custer and his cavalrymen were ordered to make a thorough reconnaissance of the country between Fort Hays and Fort McPherson on the Platte River in Nebraska.

The only recent sign of Indians that they found on that northward journey was at the Republican River. There they discovered a trail, and soon afterward they got glimpses of a small band of warriors flitting away from them and out of sight. After their arrival at Fort McPherson, they learned that a camp of Sioux, led by Pawnee Killer and other chiefs, was about 12 miles away from the post. Custer held a council meeting with them. He gave them plenty of coffee, sugar, and other similar gifts, but made no significant progress in his aim of persuading them to settle down at the military post. General Sherman, the commanding general of the army, was traveling on the new Union Pacific Railroad and visited the Custer camp at Fort McPherson. Declaring that he had no confidence in any promises made by the Indians, he urged that force was the only means to be used to control them.

The regiment's next march was to the forks of the Republican River. That the expedition was not using pack mules during this campaign is shown by Custer's statement: "At Fort McPherson we refilled our wagons with supplies of rations and forage." It is also notable that while in the Republican River country the time for sounding "taps" on the bugle was as early as 8:30 P.M., and this in the last part of June, when the hours of daylight are the longest. It appears, however, that the early-to-bed requirement was a precaution to prevent prowling Indians from seeing any lights in the camp at night.

But the Indians found them. Early one morning they made a surprise attack, the aim of which was primarily to try to stampede the soldiers' horses. But a shot fired by a picket aroused the whole camp. The frolicsome character of much of Custer's writing is exemplified in his description of himself at the time of the attack:

> General Custer on this occasion appeared in a beautiful crimson robe (red flannel *robe de nuit*), very becoming to his complexion. His hair was worn *au naturel*, and permitted to fall carelessly over his shoulders. In his hand he carried gracefully a handsome Spencer rifle. It is unnecessary to add that he became the observed of all observers.

The attacking Indians were Sioux, led by Pawnee Killer. He and Custer met to parley, but the parley was unsuccessful. The cavalrymen then chased the Indians, and there was some fighting "on the run." There were no casualties among the soldiers, but two Indians were killed.

Major Joel H. Elliott, accompanied by ten soldiers and a guide, had been sent to carry despatches to General Sherman at Fort Sedgwick, on the South Platte, in northeastern Colorado. At the same time the wagons had been sent back to Fort Wallace, Kansas, for supplies. The main body of troops did not encounter any more Indians that summer. But the wagon train's escort—a troop led by Lieutenants Cooke and Robbins—had a fight with Indians who attacked the wagon train soon after it left Fort Wallace. Another detachment of the Seventh Cavalry, led by Captain Robert M. West, hurried out to the rescue from the fort, and the Indians fled.

Seventh Cavalry officers in the 1867 campaign mentioned in Custer's book include Moylan, Weir, West, Cooke, Robbins, Elliott, Hamilton, and Dr. Coates. Some Delaware Indian scouts and a half-Cheyenne named Guerriere were with the regiment. Two white scouts especially mentioned were Will Comstock and Wild Bill Hickock.

Although the Custer soldiers had no hard fighting that summer, they saw one shocking scene that showed them what they might expect from an unsuccessful encounter with the Indians. Lieutenant Lyman S. Kidder and ten men had been sent from Fort Sedgwick to carry despatches to Custer. They did not arrive at their destination. The Custer men found all of their dead bodies—naked, with throats cut or heads cut off, bodies ripped open and bristling with projecting arrows, eyes gouged out, hands, arms, feet, or legs missing, and knife slashes all over their faces and bodies. None of the dead were individually identifiable. Some of the Seventh Cavalry officers, and probably some of the enlisted men with them, viewed at that time a sight that would be seen again nine and a half years later at the Little Bighorn, when other soldiers would look aghast on viewing their own bodies in the same horrifying state.

The campaign proper ended at Fort Wallace. Custer himself, with a small escort, pushed on first to Fort Harker, then the railhead of the Kansas Pacific Railroad, and then to Fort Riley. The main column of troops followed after.

As has already been noted, Custer, on his return, was punished on two counts—meting out unwarrantedly harsh treatment to deserters and leaving his command at Fort Wallace. Suspended from army duties and deprived of pay for one year, he spent his year of absence at his Michigan home, from which he also took some vacation trips.

No appointment was made to fill the vacancy left by Custer during his enforced absence. The regiment did some campaigning in the summer of 1868 under the leadership of General Sully, then district commander of the southern Plains region. Custer, in his book, ridiculed Sully's leadership, commenting on the fact that the commander habitually rode in an ambulance while in pursuit of the swift and elusive Indian warriors. There were no notable conflicts between the Seventh Cavalry and the Indians during this expedition.

Custer, bringing his hunting dogs with him, resumed his command early in October 1868. The main body of the regiment was then encamped on Bluff Creek, near Fort Dodge, Kansas. Just as Custer was seating himself for his first meal at the mess table, Indian warriors made one of their characteristic sudden swoops on the camp, discharging a shower of bullets and arrows before making a rapid dash away on their fleet ponies. No serious harm was done, but this and other incidents showed that the Seventh Cavalry need not expect to be idle.

A winter campaign was decided upon by General Sheridan, the department commander who had his headquarters in St. Louis. The Seventh Cavalry, scheduled to play the major role in it, was ordered to prepare. Drilling and target practice were carried out daily. A special body of sharpshooters was organized under the command of Lieutenant Cooke. All of the horses were shod, with additional front and hind shoes being made for each horse. Custer introduced the system of "coloring"—color coding—the horses in the regiment, so that there was a bay troop, a black troop, a sorrel troop, and so on. A dozen Osage Indians were employed as scouts. As autumn merged into winter, and while the soldiers waited for the Indians to settle into winter camps, some hunting trips were made.

On November 12, the regiment crossed the Arkansas River and proceeded southward. It had been decided to establish a supply base in the Indian Territory, so a train of 400 army wagons was sent out, with a few companies of infantry to serve as special guards for the wagon train. On November 18, a suitable site for a base camp was located, and the camp, named Camp Supply, was established there.

Although a snowstorm had begun to rage during the night, the intensive campaign was begun on the morning of November 23. Undeterred by the snow, the troopers mounted their horses and began their march, accompanied by wagons carrying supplies. The band took its position at the head of the column and played "The Girl I Left Behind Me." Throughout the day the storm continued, but the cavalcade made satisfactory progress despite it. The next morning the reveille was sounded at 4 A.M., after which the expedition continued its southward march under conditions that were not quite so severe.

A recent Indian trail was discovered on November 26. It led to the valley of the Washita River. Custer decided to push ahead, leaving the wagons to follow accompanied by a guard. The main body hurried forward to take up the trail. The band accompanied the troopers, who carried their sabres as well as their guns. An Indian camp was located. After waiting until night came, a final march was made, and the camp surrounded. Then the troopers waited and rested, or tried to rest, stamping their feet to keep warm until dawn came.

The command was divided into four detachments. There were 11 regular troops, with Cooke's sharpshooters making up a twelfth. With Custer's detachment, consisting of Troops A, C, D, and K, were Cooke's sharpshooters, the Osage and white scouts, and the band. When the morning light began to come, Custer made a signal to the cornetist of the brass squad. The rollicking strains of "Garryowen" burst suddenly into the frosty air. The bugles instantly sounded the charge. The battle was on.

Many Indians, of all ages, were killed, although most of them fled. The tipis and all property were burned. The Indians proved to be Southern Cheyenne, and Black Kettle, their chief, was among the dead. The outcome was rated a tremendous victory for the cavalry. But, while they were burning the camp, other

Indians arrived. These warriors captured the soldiers' overcoats and haversacks that had been left in a pile before the attack began. They came in such numbers that Custer withdrew his forces and set out on the return march for Camp Supply. It was afterwards learned that the throng of threatening warriors were from big camps of Kiowa, Arapaho, Apache, and Comanche located a few miles down the valley. It seemed quite fitting that, as the march away from the battleground was begun, the band should have played, as it did, "Ain't I Glad to Get Out of the Wilderness."

On the debit side of the expedition, 2 officers and 19 enlisted men were killed, while 3 officers and 11 enlisted men were wounded. In addition, Custer's favorite stag hound, Blucher, was riddled to death with arrows sent by the attacking warriors. Of the 21 dead men, Major Elliott and 14 men with him made up a large part. They had disappeared from the view of the main command and, at the time of the departure for Camp Supply, it was not known what had become of them. Ten days afterward, Captain George W. Yates and 100 men of the Seventh Cavalry, accompanied by Custer and Sheridan, left Camp Supply to return to the battlefield. Their purpose was partly to review the scene there, but mainly to learn for certain the fate of Elliott and his men, and to make a decent disposal of such remains as might be found. They found the remains—or rather the human debris—down the valley toward the other Indian camps. Elliott and his men had apparently been enticed into a pursuit, then ambushed and slaughtered by overpowering numbers. So, again, the men of the Seventh Cavalry beheld the sight of sickening human carnage that foreshadowed what the future held in store for their own regiment.

The campaign was resumed and continued throughout the winter. There was no bloodshed, but some satisfactory results were achieved. After much evasive parleying and dodging here and there, the Kiowa, Arapaho, and Apache were persuaded to surrender and settle down at the military posts or at the agency centers. The Cheyenne who had fled from the Washita camp went westward into the Texas Panhandle.

Early in March 1869, the Seventh Cavalry regiment left its camp ground at the site where Fort Sill was later to be established, and marched westward in search of the Cheyenne. They were accompanied by the Nineteenth Kansas Cavalry, a regiment of volunteers led by Colonel Samuel J. Crawford, who had been governor of Kansas. Together the two bodies numbered about 1,500 men.

The missing Indians were found. Two or three days of doubtful parleying and counciling ensued, with intermittent threats of battle. One incident was the return by the Cheyenne of two white women they had captured in Kansas. After every loophole of escape had been closed to them, and they saw no hope of continuing their roaming life, the Cheyenne agreed to surrender. They then followed the soldiers back to Camp Supply. This marked the end of this particular period of Indian warfare. Custer and his Seventh Cavalry were given the credit for the outcome.

Seventh Cavalry officers mentioned in Custer's book as participating in the 1868-69 campaign, or who are mentioned in Godfrey's account of the Washita battle, are the following: Custer himself, Tom Custer, Weir, Elliott, West, Hamilton, Godfrey, Mathey, Benteen, Cooke, Robbins, Yates, Beebe, Hall, Schuyler, Myers, Thompson, Gibbs, Keogh, and Drs. Renick and Lippincott. Although Captain Myles Moylan is not mentioned, it is to be presumed that he was present with the others, as he was with them in 1867 and also in subsequent years, including 1876. Captain Myles Keogh belonged to the Seventh Cavalry, but he was then on detached duty as adjutant for General Sully at his district headquarters at Fort Harker. Three scouts other than the Osage were a man named Corbin, another known simply as California Joe, and a third described by Custer as being a Negro Mexican. The third man was named Romero, but was jokingly called Romeo.

The firearms then in use by the Seventh Cavalry are mentioned by Godfrey in these words: "They were armed with the Spencer magazine carbine and Colt revolver, paper cartridges and caps." The Custer book mentions California Joe's rifle as being "a long breech-loading Springfield musket."

Elliott and Louis McLane Hamilton were the officers killed at the Washita encounter. Captain Hamilton's death occasioned special attention, as he was a grandson of the famous soldier and statesman Alexander Hamilton. Of the 20 officers mentioned as being with the Seventh Cavalry at this time, ten were still with the regiment at the Little Bighorn in 1876. They were Custer, Yates, Keogh, Tom Custer, and Cooke, all of whom were killed, and Benteen, Moylan, Weir, Godfrey, and Mathey, all of whom survived as members of the Reno-Benteen forces.

In the spring of 1871, the regiment was sent to Kentucky,

where its headquarters were established at Elizabethtown. Detachments were stationed here and there in the state or else in contiguous states. The regiment thus became a part of those United States military forces that were stationed in the South during the Reconstruction period (1865-77). Their duties were mainly to act as detectives and policemen seeking to suppress illicit distilleries as well as the Ku Klux Klan. Such duties were altogether uncongenial to Custer, and probably to his regiment as well. There was universal rejoicing when, in the early spring of 1873, orders came to move to Dakota Territory.

Steamboats took them from Memphis, Tennessee, to Cairo, Illinois, from where railroad trains transported them to Yankton, Dakota. From this point they marched up the Missouri River to Fort Rice. Here preparations were made for an expedition into the Yellowstone country of Montana. The departure from Fort Rice took place on June 21, 1873.

The purpose of the Yellowstone expedition of 1873 was to provide protection for the civil engineers making a preliminary survey for the Northern Pacific Railroad in areas then acknowledged to be Indian. General David S. Stanley was in command of the military forces, which consisted of the Seventh Cavalry under Custer and several companies of infantry. According to the writings of Godfrey, and also according to the testimony of Custer in a letter to his wife, the body of the cavalry consisted of ten troops. Two other troops were with Major Marcus A. Reno, guarding surveyors on the Canadian boundary.

A fight with the Indians occurred on August 4, at the mouth of the Tongue River. The command was marching westward at the time, up the south side of the Yellowstone Valley. Custer and a detachment were on reconnaissance some miles ahead, trying to establish the best route to travel, as was his wont. His detachment consisted of "one squadron of my command, numbering about 90 men," according to his official report. It appears that this squadron consisted of two troops, with Captain Moylan as the senior in command. Besides Moylan, the official report mentions Tom Custer, Charles A. Varnum, and James Calhoun. Calhoun, a brother-in-law of Custer, was mentioned as "my adjutant."

"The fight began at 11:30 A.M. and was waged without cessation until near three o'clock," the official report informs us. It would appear that the duration of the fight was overestimated, or else that the advance detachment was further ahead of the main command than might be supposed. The report refers vaguely to "heavy losses" by the Indians, with specific mention of five of the Indians' ponies being killed. On Custer's side, one man and two horses were wounded. During the fight, however, two civilians were killed, not far from the soldiers. This incident became the starting point of a long train of notorious events, or else of actual events which were later subjected to fictitious elaborations.

The two civilians killed were Dr. John Holzinger, a veterinary surgeon, and a man named Balarian, a sutler, both of whom were members of the expedition. These two men had left the main column to go forward, following the trail of Custer's detachment. After the battle, as the soldiers were going back towards the main column, they found the dead bodies of the two men. A year or so afterward, at Fort Abraham Lincoln, Custer got news that a Hunkpapa Sioux named Rain-in-the-Face had boasted in public that he had killed the two, or at least one of them. This report was the basis for the arrest and imprisonment of Rain-in-the-Face by the Custer brothers. The arrest and imprisonment were, in turn, the basis for the fanciful stories of a fiendish personal revenge wrought upon the Custers by Rain-in-the-Face at the Little Bighorn.

A second fight on the Yellowstone occurred on August 11. Custer and his entire command had been following the Indians they had encountered a week earlier. Not far from the mouth of Rosebud Creek the warriors took a stand to receive the soldiers. The regimental band was there, and it again played "Garryowen." There were various charges, dashes, and skirmishings. One officer, Lieutenant Charles Braden, was badly wounded. Four enlisted men, including Custer's orderly, Private Tuttle, were killed, and three enlisted men were wounded. Four cavalry horses were killed, and four were wounded. The official report estimated that 40 Indian warriors were killed. Among the officers in this second fight, the official report mentioned Yates, French, Hart, Braden, Brush, Ketchum, and McIntosh. This ended the Seventh Cavalry's fighting for the year.

During the latter part of September, the regiment returned to Fort Abraham Lincoln. This was a new post built especially for them. But it was not large enough to house all of them, so some of the troops were scattered. Custer established his headquarters at this post, and the largest detachment was kept there, but another detachment was stationed at Fort Rice, further south, and some troops were put on duty at other places. Such scattering was usual in the western Plains country, partly because there was inadequate accommodation for a full regiment at any one post, and partly because it was customary to spread out the available forces to garrison as many different points as possible, in order to increase security in local areas.

In the spring of 1874, Custer asked for orders to take the regiment somewhere in order to keep it trained in field exercises. It appears that he suggested the Black Hills country. Sheridan complied with his wishes and issued orders for an expedition to be despatched. The march was begun on July 2, 1874. By treaty agreement, the Black Hills region was Indian country. It was not to be invaded by whites, including soldiers, as long as peaceful conditions prevailed in the region. At that time conditions were entirely peaceful, so the incursion into the region was in violation of the treaty. But it was officially condoned by being given the aspect of a scientific rather than a military expedition. With the soldiers went geologists, ornithologists, and other scientific experts.

Although the purpose of the expedition was avowedly peaceful, to the Indians it may have appeared otherwise. The fact that a band of Arikara scouts accompanied the soldiers may have augmented the feeling among the Indian inhabitants of the region —mostly Northern Cheyenne, Arapaho, and Oglala Sioux—that the invasion was not a friendly one. A few long-distance shots were exchanged, on one occasion, with a small party of Cheyenne, who then fled and disappeared. This was the only semblance of armed conflict that occurred during the entire expedition. But, when all the circumstances attending the expedition are taken into account, there is ground for a suspicion that lurking in the minds of Custer and many of his followers was some such thought as: "Maybe we can stir up a war."

A variety of civilians tagged along with or after the soldiers. Boston Custer, General Custer's 17-year-old brother, was having his first experience in the western wilds. Most of the other civilians were gold prospectors. Indeed, it appears that the prospect of finding gold was the prime reason for choosing the Black Hills country as the terrain for field exercise training. Covert talk about the precious metal soon developed into unrestrained talk. On August 2, Custer wrote to his wife: "We have discovered gold, without a doubt, and probably other valuable metals."

The return to the home post was in the latter part of August. News of the discovery of gold flew to all parts of the United States. Naturally, eager white men seized their digging tools and swarmed into the Black Hills country. Soldiers from General George Crook's department of the Platte were sent to turn back the rushing human tide. But the thin barrier of their presence proved equivalent to no barrier at all. The Indians showed signs of resentment, and hostile actions were either taken or were provoked. The sprinklings of bloodshed that occurred, and the threats of much more bloodshed that were made, caused the Washington authorities to order that the Indians occupying the gold regions should be transferred to other lands. The purpose of the military was therefore changed from protecting the Indians' land to protecting the white gold prospectors, while at the same time compelling the Indians to obey the official order.

The ousting of the Indians from their lands was the basis for an incurable grudge being held by many Indians. It was also the principal ground for the resumption of the Indians' roaming, which in turn led to the military campaign of 1876. Furthermore, the cavalry regiment that played the principal role in the introductory act was also fated to play the principal role in the finale. Its members were to be cast in the role of the victims of the supreme military tragedy to be recorded in the annals of Indian frontier warfare.

Upon their return from the Black Hills expedition, the troops of the Seventh Cavalry were again scattered. They engaged in no concerted activity, nor indeed in any notable activity of any kind, until the spring of 1876, when an order came to go campaigning into the Indian hunting lands to the westward. The situation that brought on this campaign came about in the following way.

The Treaty of 1868, concluded with the Sioux and other tribes, provided for a certain area to be recognized as unceded Indian land to be used by all Indians as a hunting ground. The area was bounded on the east by the north-south line at the western edge of Dakota Territory. The 107th meridian, running north-south about 145 miles west of the Dakota line, was the western boundary. To the north the limit was the Yellowstone River, and to the south it was the North Platte River.

Some of the Indians spent all their time in this hunting land, staying away from the reservations. Others moved back and forth between the agencies and the unceded common land. The number staying away from the agencies all the time greatly increased after the ousting of the Indians from the Black Hills. It was then decided by the government authorities to abrogate the treaty clause concerning the unceded territory, and to compell all Indians roaming there to return to their reservations. A final date was set for their return, but they gave no heed to the order. The War Department was then called upon to enforce it. The military wheels began to turn. The forces ordered into the field included the Seventh Cavalry. Thus, for the third time, the Seventh Cavalry were to violate a treaty by invading Indian lands when the inhabitants were at peace. The initiative for this was, of course, not that of the Seventh Cavalry. They were dutifully obeying orders.

Messages flitted along the telegraph wires calling upon all the scattered troops to assemble at Fort Abraham Lincoln. Troops B, G, and K were in Mississippi and Louisiana. Most, or all, of the other absentees were at Fort Rice. Recruits were hurried to the regiment, in addition to those other recruits who had enlisted not long before, in order to swell the ranks to the desired strength. At this time Custer was in Washington, receiving reprimands from his superiors, and it appeared that he was not going to be allowed to lead his regiment into the field. But after his difficulties were either smoothed over or postponed, he returned to his post. It was decided that General Terry, the department commander, should lead the expedition, with Custer serving as his subordinate in command of the Seventh Cavalry. Three companies of infantry and three Gatling guns were also annexed to the force.

The regiment, consisting of 12 standard troops, left Fort Abraham Lincoln on May 17, 1876. It was accompanied by 4 Sioux and 36 Arikara scouts. Supplies were loaded into 150 wagons which, in tandem train, constituted the core of the marching formation. To one side of the wagons a herd of beef cattle was kept in motion. On the other side the pack animals, about 175 mules, were herded along. The Gatling guns were just ahead of the wagons, with the infantrymen preceding them. The cavalry troops rode to the front and the rear, at spaced distances, guarding all sides of the wagon train core. Custer and one troop always rode ahead as pathfinders through the country, much of it made up of badlands hills, and little of it ever traveled by white men before.

Major Reno and six troops of the regiment were sent from the mouth of the Powder River, a tributary of the Yellowstone, in what is now Montana to search for signs of Indians. Custer and the remaining six troops marched on up the south side of the Yellowstone to the mouth of the Tongue River, and then on to the mouth of the Rosebud. At the mouth of the Rosebud, Reno and his men returned and told of finding the Indian trail. The

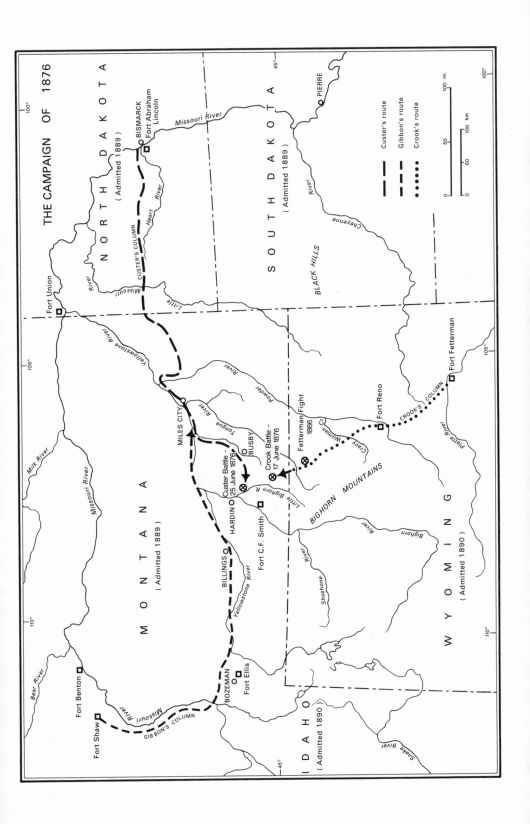

course of events after this junction of military forces is taken up later in this book.

General Godfrey, in his writings, makes special note of a striking incident which occurred when the cavalry reached the mouth of the Tongue River. There they found indications of an Indian camp that had been established during the preceding winter. In the vicinity of the campsite there were bodies of dead Indians on scaffolds or on branches of trees. The soldiers robbed the dead bodies. Godfrey, telling of the incident, expressed himself as follows:

> Several persons rode about exhibiting trinkets with as much gusto as if they were trophies of their valor, and showing no more concern for their desecration than if they had won them at a raffle. Ten days later I saw the bodies of these same persons dead, naked, and mutilated.

WHAT KIND OF SOLDIERS?

The average United States Regular Army soldier in 1876 was a man of a character quite different from that of the average United States Army soldier of contemporary times. Little care was exercised in recruiting. Discipline also appears to have been lax, although often harsh. Studies of military writings of those days reveal these weaknesses as being especially apparent in the western Plains. A few examples will illustrate the situation that then prevailed.

Custer had trouble with desertions during his first campaign on the Plains in 1867. His book, *My Life on the Plains,* tells of these difficulties. The Seventh Cavalry had just been organized and was assembled at Fort Hays, Kansas, when desertions began. Later in the summer, while the regiment was in pursuit of Indians in western Kansas and Nebraska, soldiers deserted in greater numbers. In his book, Custer attributes the defections partly to the inferior quality of the rations provided for the men, and partly to the lure of the gold fields not far away.

Forty men deserted during a single night as the Seventh Cavalry was about to leave the Platte River for the return southward. The Custer book says: "There was no time to send parties in pursuit, or the capture and return of a portion of them might have been effected." That ensuing day he learned of a general conspiracy in which "one-third of the effective strength of the command was to seize their horses and arms during the night and escape to the mountains." He took prompt steps to prevent this wholesale flight. Nevertheless, at the noon stop for rest that day, 13 soldiers joined in making a rush to get away. Seven of them were on horses, six were on foot. The seven men on horseback succeeded in escaping, but the six men on foot were pursued by Major Elliott and a body of soldiers. The pursuers caught up with the fugitives and fired upon them, "bringing down three of the deserters, although two of them were worse frightened than hurt," according to Custer.

Despite this severe measure, Custer received information that the conspiracy to desert was continuing. The move was to be made the same night that the six had been recaptured. To prevent it, he put all of his officers on all-night duty with orders to remain awake and watching. Various strict rules were promulgated in order to hinder the conspiracy. These were kept in force until the arrival of the regiment back at Fort Wallace. All of these incidents are described in full in Custer's book.

It may be that there was more difficulty about desertions in the Custer ranks in 1867 than was usual in that era. But all of the army units operating in the Plains and Rocky Mountain states had somewhat similar experiences. The rate of desertion appears to have been increased by the fact that many of the United States soldiers in the years immediately after the Civil War had been captured Confederate soldiers who had accepted service in the United States forces in order to be freed from imprisonment or, in some instances, to obtain food and other subsistence. These former Confederates were known as "galvanized" soldiers.

All through the late 1860s and the early 1870s, in practically every band of recruits sent from an assembling place to a western post, there were desertions before the post was reached. Other men deserted soon after their arrival. All such defaulters were believed to have enlisted solely to get transportation to the frontier settlements. Later, both at the posts and while on campaigns, there were more desertions. Desertions were in fact so common that, ordinarily, no effort was made to apprehend the quitters unless army equipment was taken. Even then, the pursuit was not long sustained.

The Adjutant General's report dated October 1, 1876, gives figures for desertions covering a three-year period. From June 30, 1873, to June 30, 1874, there were 4,606—about 19 percent of an army of less than 25,000. For the next year, June 30, 1874, to June 30, 1875, the number was 2,521. In the 1875-1876 period, the number was 1,832. Through ten months of this 1875-1876 year there were, according to the Judge Advocate General's report, 347 convictions for desertion.

As to other offenses during that ten-month period, the Judge Advocate General's report specifies the number of convictions as follows: offering violence to a superior officer, 6; assault with intent to kill, 10; selling, losing, or wasting government property, 140; larceny, 142; assault and battery, 214; disrespect to superiors, 289; neglect of duty, 526; disobedience of orders, 705; drunkenness on duty, 947; drunkenness, 1,568. The total number of convictions was 4,587, excluding desertions. Taken all together, this was a rather high number of culprits in an army of less than 25,000.

In the 1876 march of the Seventh Cavalry from Dakota into Montana, it appears that there were no desertions. There were many fresh recruits, and one would have presumed that among them would be the usual number of potential deserters. Possibly, either especially attractive conditions of service or else the large number of hostile Indians in the region they were traversing kept all of the soldiers in the ranks. Nonetheless, the fact that quitting without permission was not out of vogue is clear from what occurred in the ranks of General Gibbon's infantrymen. They set out from Fort Shaw in Montana Territory on March 17, 1876, to take part in the Indian war that summer. Lieutenant James H. Bradley's diary provides a daily record of events. Two men deserted from camp during the first night of their expedition. They took army horses as mounts, so it was deemed important to pursue them. This was done, and they were caught and brought back. Four days later, on March 21, the diary records another case: "It was discovered this morning that two men had deserted during the night." A third entry is dated March 27: "Lost two men by desertion last night." During the 12 days of marching from Fort Shaw to Fort Ellis, there were six deserters. Three were captured, but they were only given light punishments.

It is probable that there were many good soldiers in the Seventh Cavalry of 1876, notwithstanding their rough ways. But it is a reasonable conjecture that a considerable percentage of them were of another character. Some were simply low toughs or rowdies. Some were criminals or crooks. It was, for example, comparatively common for professional gamblers to enlist in the army for the prime purpose of practicing gambling tricks. A letter from General Godfrey to the author, written in 1929, tells of one such man. Known as Clair, he had been in the Civil War and had joined the Seventh Cavalry on its foundation in 1866. He had at first been a non-commissioned officer, but he had been demoted to private. Godfrey knew he was a gambler. On the night of June 21, at the mouth of the Rosebud River, Clair came to Godfrey's tent and asked Godfrey to accept $320 for safekeeping. After some hesitation and conversational exchange, Godfrey took the money. Four days later, Clair was killed in the Reno fight. Godfrey had some trouble in disposing of the money and finally turned it over to the army paymaster. In the letter his story ends: "Years later I learned that he had enlisted under an assumed name."

Mrs. Custer wrote of the character of the Seventh Cavalry soldiers at Fort Abraham Lincoln, where the regiment was based at the time of the fatal 1876 expedition. In her book *Boots and Saddles* she says that occasionally fugitives from justice were in the ranks. She intimates that she believed that any regiment on continuous duty in the western territories in that era afforded an inviting place for a bad man to hide himself.

General Hugh L. Scott, in *Some Memories of a Soldier* (1928), writes of the men of the Seventh Cavalry as he knew them in the autumn of 1876. He was then a lieutenant who had just left West Point. Many recruits, among whom were criminals and rough characters, had just arrived to fill the gaps in the ranks resulting from the Little Bighorn battle. There was a great deal of drunkenness and brawling by soldiers at low resorts adjoining the post. On one occasion a lieutenant and 50 men were sent to quell a big disturbance of this kind, but so many soldiers were involved in the melee that the arresting detail found themselves burdened with a heavy task. When 50 prisoners were placed in the guardhouse, there was a riot, in the course of which an attempt was made to break out, and a man was killed. According to Scott, it was later discovered that many of the men were criminals, and in consequence they were court-martialed and discharged. Scott himself was later sent to take ten convicted culprits to the federal prison at Leavenworth in the spring of 1877. The men were judged to be of such tough character that he had them shackled for the journey. He tells of a sergeant who accepted a bribe to allow a prisoner to escape and then himself deserted with the bribe-giver. The two men were captured near the Canadian border, were brought back, and were then "drummed out of service."

The achieving of full efficiency by troops stationed in Indian country on the western Plains was hindered by handicaps of various kinds. Regiments were usually scattered so that they might garrison various posts. When a campaign was to be conducted, the men were suddenly assembled and immediately sent out on combined actions for which no preparatory rehearsal as a regiment had ever been held. In 1867, in his first campaign as leader of the newly organized Seventh Cavalry, Custer had only 8 of the usual 12 troop units. He had all 12 of them, however, when he fought the Battle of the Washita in November 1868. On the Yellowstone in 1873, when he and his soldiers were guarding the railroad surveyors, he had 10 troops. During the expedition into the Black Hills in 1874, and into the same region in the spring of 1875, his forces were under the full regimental strength. But all 12 troops were with him in 1876.

During the winters between these campaigns, the troops were scattered. During the winter season immediately preceding the 1876 expedition, six troops—A, D, E, F, I, and L—were stationed at Custer's Seventh Cavalry headquarters at Fort Abraham Lincoln. Troops C, H, and M were at Fort Rice. The remaining three, Troops B, K, and G, were in Mississippi and Louisiana, where they had been for about two years. When the order came for the full regiment to take the field in the spring of 1876, all of these scattered troops assembled at Fort Abraham Lincoln. There was hurrying and hustling to get the men equipped and to get the expedition started. There was little time for the soldiers to get acquainted with each other's ways.

New recruits had been added at Fort Abraham Lincoln and at Fort Rice during the autumn of 1875. Since there is not much opportunity for cavalry training during a North Dakota winter, these men were still virtually untrained when the organization of the expedition began. Then, about a month before the start was made, 125 more newly enlisted men arrived to be transformed into instant soldiers. Thus, Custer's Seventh Cavalry, often called "the finest cavalry regiment in the service," or glorified in similar terms, consisted at the very least of 30 percent raw soldier material when it set out on that early summer day in 1876 to whip all of the Indian warriors on the Plains.

Colonel William A. Graham's book, *The Story of the Little Big Horn* (1926), quotes Edward S. Godfrey and Winfield S.

Edgerly, veteran officers who fought in the battle, as authorities for his estimate that between 30 and 40 percent of the Seventh Cavalry in combat on June 25 were raw recruits without any previous service. This was the first battle they had ever seen. He specifies that in Godfrey's Troop K there were only 17 veterans out of the total of 42 men in the troop.

At the Reno court-martial, Sergeant Ferdinand A. Culbertson, of Troop A, testified:

> Most of G Company were recruits, about half, and about a third of A Company. I don't know about M. And they had the oldest men for horseholders. The new men had very little training. They were poor horsemen and would fire at random. They were brave enough, but had not the time or opportunity to make soldiers. Some of them were not fit to take into action. About all of the instruction they had in the duties of a soldier was what Major Reno had given them that spring. Most of the time they were on some other duty that gave them no chance to learn how to fight.

Lieutenant George D. Wallace testified: "Many of the men had never been on a horse until that campaign, and they lost control of their horses when galloping into line."

The Seventh Cavalry had a reputation as an Indian-fighting regiment. But, prior to June 25, 1876, when had they fought Indians? Their only major engagement had been almost eight years before, in November 1868, at the Washita. In 1867 there had been two encounters, with no fatalities among the soldiers. On the Yellowstone in 1873, there had been one fight in which four soldiers had been killed, and a second fight in which one soldier had been killed. There had been no other contested encounters. In 1876, therefore, even the veterans in service could not claim much experience in actually fighting Indians, unless they were among the superveterans whose service went back eight years to the Washita.

The Seventh Cavalry's officers in 1876 were: General Custer; Major Reno; Captains Benteen, Yates, Keogh, Tom Custer, Moylan, Weir, French, and McDougall; Lieutenants Cooke, Godfrey, Calhoun, Smith, Reilly, Sturgis, Porter, Harrington, Hodgson, Edgerly, Wallace, McIntosh, Gibson, DeRudio, Varnum, Hare, and Mathey, with Lieutenant Crittenden, an infantry officer, temporarily attached. Of these 28 officers, nine had been in the Washita battle. These nine were: General Custer; Captains Benteen, Yates, Moylan, Weir, and Tom Custer; and Lieutenants

Cooke, Godfrey, and Mathey. The same nine were in the 1873 fight, and, in addition, Captain French and Lieutenants Varnum, Calhoun, and McIntosh had been there. The 15 other officers at the Little Bighorn—more than half of the total number—had never before been in any kind of fight against the Indians in which any actual resistance had been made.

Of the 12 officers in the Custer detachment at the Little Bighorn four were Washita superveterans—General Custer, Captains Yates and Tom Custer, and Lieutenant Cooke. Calhoun, an 1873 veteran, was also with them. Among the 16 officers of the combined Reno-Benteen forces on the entrenched hill at Little Bighorn were five Washita superveterans—Benteen, Moylan, Weir, Godfrey, and Mathey. With them also were Varnum and McIntosh, 1873 veterans. In the valley, Reno had one Washita superveteran —Moylan—and two 1873 veterans—Varnum and McIntosh. Lieutenant Mathey, who had been with the wagon train at the Washita, was with the mule pack train at the Little Bighorn. Under these circumstances, one understands more clearly why Reno was gladdened by the arrival of the Benteen men and the pack mules. Reno knew that Benteen, Weir, Godfrey, and Mathey—four old-time Washita officers—would be able to help in steadying the wrecked remnants of his cavalry detachment.

In the Seventh Cavalry as it was in 1876, the figure for officer inexperience in contested battle against Indians may be reasonably fixed at about 55 percent. The percentage of inexperienced enlisted men may reasonably be raised considerably, since officers were usually in the army as a lifetime vocation, while comparatively few enlisted men stayed for any long term of years. Further, the large number of men who had enlisted just before the 1876 campaign raised the inexperience percentage to a much higher figure. While no precise percentage can be calculated, it seems reasonable to estimate that three-fourths or more of the men had never before seen a hostile Indian painted up and ready to fight until, on that memorable day, there suddenly loomed up in front of them and all around them hundreds and thousands of such warriors.

General Godfrey, in the years immediately preceding his death in 1932, wrote various long and enlightening letters to the author. Commonly, they were in reply to queries concerning the Custer battle or matters connected with it. In one such letter, in reply to a question as to the presence of new recruits and other inexperienced men being a factor in the Custer catastrophe, the General wrote on February 13, 1929: "It is my impression that most of the men were in their first fight on June 25th. Yes, I do think this was an important factor in the defeat."

Major Reno and the three troops with him, accompanied by the Arikara and Crow Indian scouts, were sent to make the first charge upon the Indian camps. They were met by a large number of warriors. The soldiers dismounted, fought for a few minutes lying flat on the ground, then sought shelter in a patch of timber. After a short time spent fighting in the timber, they fled towards and across the river to a hilltop refuge. Those who have since reviewed that swift movement all agree that the men were in a panic flight.

The attempt to place the responsibility for that wild scramble in search of security led to the blame falling upon Major Reno. There was little open discussion of the revealing fact that all of the officers and most of the enlisted men with Reno were in a situation that was not only entirely new to them but also peculiarly terrifying, even to the experienced men. Although derogatory criticism of the conduct of the whole detachment was usually subdued or suppressed, some of it did find open expression. Some of it came out in the form of testimony at Major Reno's court-martial. At that trial, Reno's conduct was fully discussed, and the entire course of such fighting as took place under his direction was reviewed. No such inquiry was made concerning the conduct of Custer and his detachment at that time, since for that purpose there were no surviving witnesses to give testimony, unless the Indians who had fought against him had been produced. Nevertheless, the actions of the men under Reno may in all probability be considered as exemplifying the actions of the men with Custer.

In addition to the previously quoted testimony at the Reno trial, George Herendeen, a scout with Reno, told of the excitement which spread among the men. Telling of the rush by the Reno men to get away from the Indians in the valley, he said: "I saw no shots fired by the men as they ran. I saw one of them throw away his gun as he left the timber. He was afoot and he was left behind."

Lieutenant DeRudio testified that his G Troop "appeared to be in a panic." He tried to calm them and to keep them all together so that they might leave the timber in the proper form, but they all quit and left him there. He remained hidden in that timber thicket and elsewhere along the river throughout that night, all the next day, and until the last part of the following night, by which time all the Indians had gone.

Captain Frederick W. Benteen's official report on his south-

ward detour reveals his thoughts concerning the inexperience of
the soldiers. He was returning from his detour, with Troops H,
D, and K, when he saw the Reno men fighting in the valley. He
was about to join them, but he saw that they were in retreat and
apparently being routed, and was deterred from going to their
assistance by thoughts of "the large element of recruits" among his
own men. He judged that they "would stand no earthly chance"
in an encounter with the Indians.

E. A. Brininstool's writings contain some narratives by veterans
who were with the Reno-Benteen forces. One of these narrators
was the aged Colonel Varnum, who had been a lieutenant in 1876.
Varnum told Brininstool: "On the retreat almost everybody I saw
was considerably excited. They were in that condition when they
went into the engagement, for that matter." At another point
in his narrative he said: "I saw a good many excited men shooting
right up in the air."

Another participant, William C. Slaper, tells his story in
Brininstool's *A Trooper With Custer* (1925). He was a private
in Captain Thomas French's Troop M. He had enlisted, aged 20,
in September 1875. He had six weeks of training at Jefferson
Barracks in St. Louis, Missouri, and was then sent to Fort Abraham Lincoln. He tells of having had "no experience in roughing
it, much less of Indian fighting." As to his own conduct during the
fight in the valley:

> I remember that I ducked my head and tried to dodge bul-
> lets which I could hear whizzing through the air. This was
> my first experience under fire. I know that for a time I was
> frightened, and far more so when I got my first glimpse of
> the Indians riding about in all directions and firing at us and
> yelling and whooping like incarnate fiends, all seemingly as
> naked as the day they were born, and painted from head to
> foot in the most hideous manner possible.

Private Slaper's feelings may be taken as expressing those of
practically all the other inexperienced soldiers who took part in
either the fight in the valley or the fight on Custer ridge. The combined Reno-Benteen forces on the hilltop fought a steady battle
for many hours later in the day, and for many more hours the next
day. But before the fighting began on the hilltop, the soldiers
had about two hours in which to calm themselves, to organize
resistance, to corral their horses and mules inside their lines, and
to prepare themselves in every way for the coming Indian onslaught. Custer and his men had no such opportunity. Their situa-

tion was similar to that of the Reno men in the valley. In approaching the Indian camps, they saw an astounding flood of warriors coming out to meet them. It is reasonable to believe that the conduct of the Custer soldiers was much the same as that of the Reno men when the Indians first swept down on them.

It is also enlightening to contrast the caliber of the composite Seventh Cavalry forces with that of the Indians who fought against them. Every one of the Indian warriors had been a horseman—had almost lived on horseback—since he had been a small boy. Every one of them had been receiving training as a warrior since early youth. Almost all of them had been in previous battles, either against white people or against antagonists of their own race. Instead of the 80 percent inexperience rate found among the white soldiers, the percentage of experience among the Indians may fairly be estimated at more than 80 percent. It was an experience, moreover, which generated cool efficiency in mortal combat. Ignoring the great difference in numbers, and measuring the opposing forces man for man, it would seem that the Indians deserve distinctly the higher rating. They were skilled fighters who knew what to do in combat, and who did it.

INDIAN WARRIOR WAYS

Lack of knowledge of the Indian concepts of warfare is evident in many of our published accounts of battles in which they participated. Descriptions of their battles are often characterized by the same pompous and stilted terminology commonly used to describe our own military movements. Their aims in armed encounters have been presumed to be the same as our. Errors of understanding have occurred because the actions of the Indian warriors have been measured by our standards, instead of theirs.

But the Indian system of warfare had roots and flowerings quite different from ours—as different, indeed, as their entire system of thought. Warfare, as they practiced it, varied in its details, but its basic roots were common to all the North American tribes. In order to understand any battles that they fought, it is necessary to know something of their characteristic ideas concerning combat. In order to understand the Custer battle in particular, it is best to focus attention upon the military aims and methods of the western Plains tribes, especially the Sioux and Cheyenne, since it was they who opposed Custer.

The warrior societies of each tribe constituted its military forces. Ordinarily, a tribe had three or four such organizations. Membership was by invitation complemented by voluntary choice. In fighting their tribal enemies, the societies were in constant rivalry, seeking to outdo one another in the performance of deeds of valor. A war party seeking combat was regularly composed of members of only one of the societies, and those who were nonmembers of any society were excluded. When large numbers of enemies made an attack—as was the case at the Little Bighorn—the warrior societies, or groups from these societies, took turns at showing what they could do. Under such circumstances it was not customary for all warriors in the tribe to be fighting at the same time, for this would have greatly hindered competition between the societies. Individual members of a society also competed among themselves. Indeed, the manifestation of individuality in action—personal exhibitions of bravery and cunning—was the prime consideration.

Rivalry between the different warrior societies was not confined only to warfare, but was extended to include all kinds of other manly activities. For example, members of one society would try to outdo the others on hunting expeditions. Societies were matched against each other in athletic contests. They also competed in scouting, in accumulating ponies, and in having good tipis and fine clothing. Gentle decorum and certain character traits of various kinds were regarded as creditable, and such traits were fostered by each of the societies. Individuals within each society strove to win honors in their own segregated circle. Thus, the meshing of all competition between individuals as well as between the societies encouraged those virtues which strengthened the tribe.

The ages for the beginning and end of an individual's service as a warrior were usually not precisely fixed. James Willard Schultz, author of *William Jackson, Indian Scout* (1926), wrote that among the Blackfeet the warrior period lasted from the ages of 15 to 37. The Sioux generally considered 37 as the proper age to give up aggressive warrior activity. The Cheyenne had no established limits, but followed what might be termed a "common law" rule among Indians—that each tipi household should have at least one warrior, or else it would lose social prestige. Each young husband continued to be a warrior until he had a son old enough to fight, and hence to become the family tipi's representative. If no natural son was available by the time a warrior reached a fitting retirement age, a son was adopted. The adopted son might be either an orphan or the male offspring of some relative or friend who had a surplus of sons.

Each warrior society elected its own leading chief as well as its subsidiary chiefs, or "little chiefs." Among the Cheyenne, the standard number of little chiefs for each warrior society was nine. The Cheyenne had three warrior societies in their tribe at the time of the Custer battle, while each Sioux tribe there had three or four. There were altogether five Sioux tribes as well as the Northern Cheyenne tribe in the great aggregation of camps beside the Little Bighorn. Since the Cheyenne tribe had three warrior societies, with a total of 3 leading warrior chiefs and 27 little warrior chiefs, it may be estimated that for all the six tribes the total was about 20 leading warrior chiefs and 180 little warrior chiefs.

The warrior chiefs were officials merely within their various warrior societies. They were not chiefs in the tribal governing body. Ordinarily, the warrior chiefs were in the later years of their young manhood. Tribal chiefs, on the other hand, were generally middle-aged or older men, and the oldest among them commonly held the highest rank. In rare instances, a warrior chief was also a tribal chief, but the two offices were not connected. Often a warrior chief was made a tribal chief after his warrior days had passed, but there were many tribal chiefs who had not been warrior chiefs at all.

Chiefs of warrior societies were instructors or advisors, not commanders. Instruction was imparted during times of quiet, whether at society meetings or in usual daily associations. In times of battle, such a chief would shout advice or set an example for his own immediate followers. In addition, old men past their fighting years posted themselves in the background and called out advice—whether to an individual, to a group, or to all of the fighting men. An uninformed observer might have supposed that there were many commanding officers directing operations. In fact, nobody was commanding. Individual warriors accepted or rejected, as they chose, whatever advice was offered. Any one of them was free to decide for himself that this was not his lucky day for fighting, after which he would quit and leave the field. The only penalty for such action was a social shaming if it was adjudged that his excuse for withdrawal was flimsy.

One or another of the warrior societies, or else a group of members from it, was on duty at all times in the role of policemen, or "soldiers," for the tribe. In some tribes such a group formed a semipermanent regular army, but in most tribes the duty was shifted from time to time, so that different societies served at different times. Thus, each group competed for honors in displaying its efficiency in its tribal soldier role. The assignment of duty was made by the tribal chiefs in council. Merits and demerits were also discussed there, and long or short terms of service were decreed, in accordance with what was judged to be in the best interests of the tribe. These appointed Indian soldiers kept the tribe in proper order during times of traveling. The soldiers also compelled obedience to tribal rules about hunting, and they enforced laws in camp. As special camp guards, they were also responsible for meeting any enemy attack promptly. Those who were on intensive duty as camp guards kept ponies picketed near the tipis and kept themselves otherwise ready to hurry out to fight. Thus, they acted as "shock troops," shielding the tribe from attackers until full resistance could be made or until the people could escape.

The term "dog soldier" was applied to an individual serving his turn as a tribal policeman. It seems the designation arose from the Indian sense of humor, the policeman being fancied as in alliance with the dogs in guarding against any intrusion by strangers. But the position of dog soldier was not seen as meriting derision. On the contrary, it was regarded as a specially honorable one. In some tribes it was the custom for the dog soldier to wear a rawhide lariat around his body. It was a rather short lariat and had a picket pin tied to its end. In case duty required him to take a stand, the soldier let out his length of lariat from his body and drove the picket pin into the ground. There, within the radius of a small circle, he stood as an obstacle to aggression. Having taken his stand, it was not permissible for him to draw out the pin in order to escape danger. He must stay on the spot, to die, if death should come to him, unless a soldier companion should adjudge him to be unnecessarily endangered, in which case he would come to his aid by pulling up the picket pin or cutting the rope.

To show bravery—preferably without being obliged to do any killing—was the Indian warrior's paramount aim. Scalps or dead bodies of enemies were often exhibited as circumstantial evidence of bravery, but they were not regarded as conclusive proof of merit. The degree of risk a warrior took, not the devastation he wrought, brought him the honor he coveted. Some credit was accorded for stealing from the enemy a marriageable young woman, a child, or a desirable article of property, especially a horse. But higher credit was won by incurring the greater risks run in a personal encounter with a warrior enemy.

The "touch" upon an enemy's person, to which we apply the French word *coup*, was credited as a genuine honor score for the aggressor. It might be merely a touch, as it often was, or it might be an actual maiming or disabling blow, but the credit was the same. The touch had to be by the hand or else by something— a knife, a club, or a spear—held in the hand and used only at close quarters. Often, a slender wand was carried for this particular purpose. Either the handle or the lash of a pony whip was an instrument of touch in common use. The idea was not to disable, but to insult, so that when a light instrument was used the bravery shown was held to be the greater. If the touched one resented the insult, and a hand-to-hand fight ensued, the contesting warriors were accorded equal honors, regardless of which one might kill the other.

An arrow or a bullet, which was shot at an antagonist with whom one was not in immediate contact, and which hit and even killed him, did not count as an honor score. In such cases, if the victim fell down, and if the enemy warriors saw him fall, there was usually a rush to get to the body. The one who arrived first and touched the body gained the prime honor. The second, third, and fourth touchings were credited as honors of second, third, and fourth rank. After the fourth man, there were no further creditings.

Credit for bravery for having touched the dead body of an enemy might not seem well founded. But, as the Indians explained it, the supposed dead enemy might not be dead, and might be only slightly injured, or even not injured at all. Sometimes a warrior might cunningly feign death in order to lure some overeager or gullible antagoinst over to him in order to inflict a blow that might perhaps be fatal. This was a characteristic warrior trick that was often attempted and that occasionally succeeded. In other instances death was feigned in order to obtain immunity from further attack and to gain time to wriggle away to a safer position from which a counterattack could later be made. In Indian warfare, therefore, to rush forward and touch a fallen enemy was justly accounted as a brave deed.

In many instances cleverness, as much as bravery, was a factor. The Crow Indians tell of a certain chief among them who had gained numerous warrior coups, most of which he had won by his sagacity. When participating in a battle, he remained mounted on his swift pony, peeping out from behind some shelter while his companions did most of the shooting. When he saw an enemy fall, he lashed his pony and dashed forward to make the first coup touch. The man who had sent the fatal bullet or arrow was not, however, accorded any honor for his deed.

Youths, and sometimes small boys, also made coup touches

upon enemy dead. If a battle afforded them the opportunity, they posted themselves at a safe distance and watched its progress. Old men regularly attended such youths and boys to stimulate their ambition—or else, in many instances, to restrain them from taking foolish risks. At the end of the battle, and at times during its progress, they rushed forward to touch, strike, cut, or shoot an arrow into the inert flesh of fallen enemies.

A warrior making a coup touch shouted out an announcement of his act. In this way he drew the attention of his companions who thus became his witnesses. His shout also notified the enemy, if living. Claims to coup honors were decided at councils of chiefs, where they had to be corroborated by sufficient evidence. Having been allowed his claim, the warrior could thereafter stand up in public assemblies and boast of his deed. On such occasions his witnesses, if present, called out their corroborative affirmations. Accredited touches on four different occasions were required in order to gain full recognition as an accomplished warrior. In the case of a youth, four boy coups were required to qualify him for membership in a warrior society.

The most highly honored coup act was that of disarming an enemy without doing any serious physical injury to him. Every Indian warrior therefore sought to wriggle, squirm, dodge, or rush suddenly upon an enemy, wrest his weapon from him, and escape with his own life. Such a deed established the victorious warrior's reputation throughout the remainder of his life as an admirably humane man as well as a very brave one. It was as if by such a deed he had said: "I now have your weapon. I could kill you, without danger to myself. But that would not be a brave act, so I choose not to do so."

The act of killing, under any circumstances, was never rated as a credit to a warrior. During his career, he might of course kill many enemies, but such acts were performed in retaliation, or out of rapacity, or in self-defense. They were not in themselves regarded as brave acts. The warrior had preserved himself, had wreaked vengeance, or had obtained property—in each case for a motive of selfish origin. Every killing was therefore penalized instead of being praised. Each warrior who killed somebody, even if it was an enemy attacking his tribe, accompanied the act of killing with a death-wail prayer for forgiveness by the Everywhere Spirit.

Our published narratives of Indian battles often mention a "yell of triumph" by a warrior just as he crashed his tomahawk into a victim's head. But the yell was not one of triumph. It was the death-wail. Our writings also describe instances when a war-rior received a death wound and "let out a yell"—supposedly a shriek of terror—just as he fell. But this cry was also a death-wail, a prayer by the dying man for his own soul. This weird outcry was also emitted in chorus whenever a general charge was made against enemy forces. At such times it was expected that death would surely strike someone, so that the wail was for either enemy or friend. The death-wail may still be heard on the reservations, whenever a death occurs or is imminent. For the prayer is made when any soul parts from the body, in peace no less than in war.

In Mrs. Custer's *Boots and Saddles,* she tells of the behavior of the Arikara Indian scouts as they were about to leave with the Seventh Cavalry on the 1876 expedition. They held a ceremony in which they beat drums and rode about while singing what she—as other writers have done in similar cases—supposed to be their "war songs." As most whites would have done, Mrs. Custer regarded these proceedings as intended to instill courage, as, in effect, constituting a kind of "pep" meeting. But she then goes on to say that the music was rather depressing, with the songs appearing to be more of a lament or dirge, prayers for the prospective dead.

The Arikara went through the same proceedings on the morn-ing of the Little Bighorn battle, as the Seventh Cavalry column was leaving the divide to go down to attack the Indians in the camps. The reports concerning this incident are usually written in derisive or farcical vein. The Osage Indian scouts who served with Custer in 1868 made similar preparations before the Battle of the Washita. Custer's book exhibits his amusement at their funny "medicine making." To the Indians, however, such occa-sions were as solemn as those upon which George Washington "made medicine" in his prayers at Valley Forge, or when Stone-wall Jackson, in the same way, "made medicine" every time before he went into battle.

Orin Grant Libby's *The Arikara Narrative of the Campaign Against the Hostile Dakotas, 1876* (1920) tells something in this regard of Indian actions during the course of a battle. Several Arikara, including Young Hawk, were with the Reno soldiers in the exciting mix-up in the valley. Some of them got into a segre-gated conflict with a party of Sioux who came up around them. One Sioux had tumbled from his pony and was being dragged by the animal. The Arikara fire was then directed at the pony. One of the Arikara, telling Dr. Libby about it, said: "Young

Hawk fired twice at the horse and at last killed him. As the horse fell, Young Hawk gave the Arikara yell which is always given at the death of an enemy." The published term "Arikara yell" might be construed as not referring to the death-wail. But, as the story goes on, it becomes plain that such a meaning is in fact intended. Soon after this incident, another one occurred in which the same Young Hawk took part. In the book he tells: "I saw one Sioux coming right toward me, and I drew a fine bead on him and dropped him, then I jumped up and gave the death call again."

Much of the soul-cleansing procedure—"medicine making"— was carried out after the event by any Indian who had at any time caused the death of a human being. He went into mourning, exhibiting such tokens and generally conducting himself as his tribal customs required. Dr. Charles Eastman, the Sioux Indian physician and author, wrote that among his people the period of such mourning by a man who had killed another was for 30 days. During that time he kept his face blackened, left his hair flowing loose and unkempt, and neglected all care of his personal appearance. He totally refrained from all the customary activities of his daily life, except those which were necessary for self-preservation.

The feeling of awe at taking human life was also felt—probably to a lesser degree—when animals were killed. It also extended to vegetation and, indeed, to all life. Grass or trees might be cut without offense, but if any were uprooted an apology and explanation were due, and a prayer for forgiveness by the Everywhere Spirit was made. The hunter asked for divine permission before he went after buffalo or other game, and killed only what he needed. The author has witnessed on various occasions the killing of beef by Indians when agency rations were issued. The butchering was preceded by Indian religious ceremonies—"making medicine." The occasion was a solemn one. The organization of the butchering was methodical, with different persons being assigned to perform the various actions required. The leader stood up and made a prayer. As each beef was brought into the killing pen, the leader addressed it, explaining that it was needed for human food and asking its forgiveness for the fatal act about to be committed.

Purity of character—according to the Indian standard—was essential for the Indian who would become a great warrior. If a band planned to go on a war party to seek adventure, they "made medicine" beforehand in order to ensure success or, perhaps, to prepare for the death that might result. Preparatory religious exercises included a sweat bath taken under the direction of a tribal spiritual leader, or medicine man. The party usually left the home camp and stayed away for a day or so while completing the ceremonies. Young men and husbands joining a war party symbolically "threw away" sweethearts or wives. In theory, during the entire expedition, there were no thoughts of any women. In fact, no mention of them was allowed. Indecency or vulgarity of speech that might have been permissible as adding spice to conversation in peacetime was utterly taboo in a war party.

The splendid costumes and the facial paintings of warriors going into battle were not "war regalia," as we commonly term them. Standing Bear, the Oglala Sioux author, emphatically states the truth that an old-time Indian had no such articles as a "war shirt." He would, however, dress for battle in his finest clothes, if he had time to make such preparation. When a warrior went "on the warpath" he took with him, in a rawhide bag, all of his richest clothing. But the forethought was of possible death. The costume and the facial paintings were for death and burial, not for combat. The purpose was to present a handsome and respectable appearance if taken from this world into the presence of the Everywhere Spirit. Old Indians still treasure these "war regalia" costumes, which they wear on special occasions, such as parades. But every one of them considers the outfit solely as his death and burial attire, intended for use at the time of his death. Such, indeed, always was their destined function.

Quite frequently, in times of warfare, one warrior or another would leave off his fine clothing, strip naked, and paint his body in a "medicine" way supposed to render him invulnerable to enemy fire. He left off his death and burial clothing as a token of his firm belief in his own invulnerability, his positive conviction that he was not gong to die that day. Such warriors, fortified by their belief, exposed themselves in defiant manner while others crept about, dodging from hiding place to hiding place, or keeping themselves sheltered in the usual Indian manner. Many white narrators of battles against the Indians tell of the "naked and hideously painted savages" confronting them. In fact, the naked warriors were the ones that they saw most clearly, since they held themselves in plain view all the time. Commonly, if it was a pitched battle with Indians surrounding the whites, the white men did not see many of the other warriors, except when heads would bob up from time to time. Thus, the readers of such stories, deceived in the same way that the narrators were, have supposed that the Indians usually fought naked.

The gorgeous feathered warbonnet was a badge signifying warrior accomplishment. Commonly, it was not worn until after some years of fighting experience had been gained. The time for assuming it was decided by each individual, according to his own appraisal of his merit. But if some young man too presumptuously bloomed out in a warbonnet, or if some older warrior wore it before popular opinion acclaimed him as worthy, he would be ridiculed into holding his vanity in check. The warrior who wore the bonnet proclaimed thereby that he regarded himself firstly as adept in fighting, and secondly as having full knowledge of the ethics of mortal combat.

Indian warriors were governed by a code of ethics. There was much more mutual courtesy among them than most white writers on the subject have indicated. Their chivalry may be compared with the chivalry of medieval Europe, when knights rode to do battle in tournaments. The old Indian stories provide many examples of this, of which a conspicuous one is found in the writings of Standing Bear. In sketch form, it runs as follows:

A battle was being fought between Sioux and Pawnee warriors. One Pawnee, holding his bow and arrows, stood forth and challenged the Sioux. A Sioux horseman dashed past him and touched him with a lance. In return, the Sioux was wounded by an arrow from the Pawnee's bow. A second Sioux sallied forth, struck the same sort of blow, and also received an arrow wound in return. A third Sioux and a fourth both administered blows and received wounds in the same way. This made four coup touches on the Pawnee, for each of which he obtained revenge. The warrior honors were even. At this point, the combined Sioux group could have killed the Pawnee. But they had obtained all the warrior honors obtainable from him, and to kill him would not only have been superfluous but would also have been, according to the Indian code of ethics, the dastardly slaughtering of a brave man. Instead, the four Sioux rode away, leaving the Pawnee unharmed.

James Willard Schultz, who lived for many years among the Piegan Blackfeet Indians, tells of a Crow man and boy held in captivity by the Blackfeet. The man was assigned various difficult feats to perform, to show what bravery and skill he might possess. Satisfactory performance was to be rewarded with liberty for himself and the boy. Failure in any instance was to be penal-

ized by the killing of both of them. Test after test was met successfully. The final test was a death duel with a Blackfeet man
whose warrior days were past, but who had expressed a desire
to die in battle rather than peacefully. The duel took place. The
Crow killed the Blackfeet veteran warrior. Whereupon the throng
of Blackfeet spectators cheered the Crow for his bravery, gave
him the dead veteran's horse and war accouterments, gave the
boy a horse, supplied both of them with plenty of food, and
provided them with every comfort for their journey back to their
own people.

Standing Bear, in his writings, describes the Indian treatment
of captives that was customary when he was a small boy. Some
warriors of his tribe, the Oglala Sioux, captured a small band
of Pawnee men, women, and children. After a short period of
detention, the captives were invited to a feast. When the feast
was ended, every one of the captives was given a pony and plenty
of food, and all were released to return to the Pawnee camp.
Some years later, when Standing Bear had grown to manhood,
he went as a student to the Carlisle Indian School at Carlisle,
Pennsylvania. Here he met and renewed acquaintance with a
young Pawnee who as a boy had been one of the captive party.

A certain old Crow Indian acquaintance of the author is listed
on the Crow agency roll under the name of Robert Half. Indian
surnames—that is to say the original Indian names—are often
abbreviated or imperfectly translated either for agency roll convenience or for the general convenience of whites. Knowing
this, the author requested the old man to explain his brief sur-
name, "Half." In explanation, he told a story:

In the 1860s, when Robert Half was a small boy, the Crow
tribal camp was, on a certain occasion, pitched on the north side
of the Yellowstone River, on what later became the fairground
at Billings, Montana. One day, out in the hills to the northward,
some Crow scouts from the camp saw a long line of Indians walking in the distance in single file. A count disclosed that there were
50 of them approaching the Crow camp. They were identified
as Piegan Blackfeet, a tribe constantly at war with the Crow,
and it was evident that they were planning to raid the Crow pony
herds.

The Crow scouts hurried to the camp and reported what they
had seen. Heralds rode about on horseback and notified the whole
camp. That night the pony herds were specially guarded. No
raiders appeared, however. The next morning a large party of
Crow warriors sallied forth to search for human trails in order

to find out what might have become of the Piegan. The invaders were tracked to a shallow cave in the side of a high cliff not far from the camp. A battle began which lasted for several hours. Then a Piegan appeared in plain view and made peace signs. He informed the Crow that half of the Piegan had been killed, and that the remaining half was willing to surrender.

The 25 Piegan prisoners were escorted to the Crow camp. The Crow women loaded pots and kettles with meat and began to cook them on their fires. The prisoners, with downcast countenances, were seated in a circle. Meat was set before them until they had eaten their fill. Then the Crow chiefs joined them. The ceremonial pipe was lighted and was ritually passed around the circle for a communal smoke. Young Crow then rounded up a band of their ponies and drove them to the prison tipi. Each Piegan was allowed to select a gift pony for himself. Each was also given a liberal supply of food. All of them were then granted their full freedom and, mounted on their ponies, started for home.

Such hospitality was in conformity with the Indian warrior code. Many similar examples which occurred in the course of intertribal warfare might be cited. The standard rule was that when, in matched battle, one half of a band of warriors was killed, the remaining half was permitted to surrender. The treatment accorded to the Piegan prisoners in the Crow-Piegan incident was standard. Warriors thus released were "on parole," as we might term it, as it was considered that they owed their lives to the generosity of their captors. The released men were therefore in honor bound never again to make war upon the people who had spared them. Because of this condition, it often happened that offers of good treatment in return for surrendering were refused, the surviving half of the warriors preferring to die fighting rather than to bind themselves never again to make war against their enemies. The original name of Robert Half, given him to mark this particular occasion, was not, as abbreviated, "Half," but "Half of Them Killed and Half of Them Go Free."

General Hugh L. Scott spent a large part of his military career among the western Plains Indians, as well as among the Moros on the Philippine island of Sulu. His book, *Some Memories of a Soldier,* makes comparisons between the lifestyles of these two peoples and finds many similarities in their warrior ways. Of the Plains Indians he writes: "Often I found in them traits of chivalry, of ethical consciousness, of spirituality and philosophy that I suspected were superior sometimes to the equivalent qualities in us."

Great losses by the Indians in battles where their warriors

surrounded whites, especially professional soldiers, have been reported by practically all writers who have told of such encounters. But as a matter of course these reports may be heavily discounted. The number of warriors killed was usually only a fraction of the number of losses indicated by white writers. Doubtless, some of these stories of heavy losses are conscious exaggerations made in order to reflect additional credit upon the narrator, or to convey a general impression of white superiority. But in other instances the overestimating results from a lack of knowledge of Indian ways. The outcome of an Indian charge, for example, whether on horseback or on foot, was often deceptive. If the defending white men fired enough bullets to threaten serious harm, warriors came tumbling down from their ponies, or, if on foot, they fell sprawling forward. Then, usually untouched by any bullet, they wriggled back along the ground to a safe retreat. Or again, if conditions seemed appropriate, one such "fallen" warrior would feign death in order to lure an unsuspecting enemy toward him, while at the same time holding himself in readiness to inflict a disabling blow upon his adversary.

Warrior leaders were held to rigid account for the losses of followers in battle. Often, upon returning to his home camp, a leader of a war party would be bitterly upbraided by women mourners. If there had been gross negligence in allowing young men to take risks, the leader faced a penalty, such as having his ponies killed, his tipi torn down, or his property of other kinds destroyed. Thus, there was an incentive to exercise caution in battle.

The loss of only a few warriors, and perhaps even only one, might cause a party of attackers to decide that their "medicine" was not working right, and that it would be better to retire. The result of the initial charge often determined the outcome of a battle. Indians never made repeated charges, despite losses, as white military men have often done in order to gain some fixed objective. Indians did not share white ideas about the value of such an "objective." In the battle stories told by Indian narrators to the author, it has been common for a reference to the killing of one or two members of the attacking party to be followed by the phrase: "So that ended the fight."

All of the mass killings of Indians by whites have occurred when the Indians were surprised in camp and could not escape. It may be confidently assumed that there was never any big killing of Indian warriors when the Indians were the attackers, since under such circumstances the Indians were able to withdraw whenever they chose to do so.

Various writers, in past times, have commented on these characteristically Indian ways of warfare, noting that they usually resulted in losses being low in number. Theodore Roosevelt's *Winning of the West*, for example, contains a thorough exposition of the subject. He also cites many preceding authorities to sustain his opinions, which contradict the usual braggadocio accounts of the heavy losses suffered by the Indians in battles with white soldiers. In early colonial times and in the frontier era which followed, he maintains that instead of the Indians outnumbering the white forces, as was commonly claimed, the truth was that the whites usually outnumbered the Indians. He also declares his belief that as individuals the Indians were the better fighters and that, in battles in which the two opposing forces were approximately equal in number, the white losses were much greater than those of the Indians. He relates that a Sioux Indian warrior told him that the Indian idea was to retreat from any engagement in which it became apparent that, even though a victory might ultimately be gained by the Indians, there would be the probability of heavy losses.

It has for long been a standard practice to depict Indian warriors as scalping and mutilating dead bodies, and as being eager to take prisoners in order to torture them by burning them at the stake or skinning them alive. It was in fact a common practice to mutilate dead bodies and to take scalps. Some authorities claim that scalping was taught to the Indians by the French and British colonials, who enlisted Indian aid on their respective sides in their American conflicts. Whatever its origin, however, scalping became known as a deed of valor that was peculiarly Indian in character. But there were also many white frontiersmen who adopted it in their warfare against Indians, as is clear from many of our frontier stories. One instance which occurred at the Little Bighorn battle came to light at the Reno court-martial trial. Lieutenant Edgerly was testifying about the actions of Reno and his men as they fled from the valley to the hilltop. In his testimony he said: "I remember one man who was perfectly cool and came up the hill holding a scalp he had taken."

Representations that there were scalp dances or other jubilations in the Indian camps on the night after the Custer battle are false. Indians never rejoiced over killings. Instead, the participating warriors went into mourning at once. Moreover, that night many Indian families were sorrowing over their own dead, and they were certainly in no mood for jubilation. As for scalp dancing, this was usually an affair in which only women participated. It was habitually held before, not after, a battle. Such dances were held for the purpose of stirring up martial enthusiasm among the warriors and, in the course of them, the women relatives of those who had taken the scalps exhibited them as evidence of what their kinsmen had done. Whatever turmoil might have been observed in the Indian camps the night after the Custer battle was due to causes not in the least connected with scalp dancing or celebrations. It most probably arose from feelings the very opposite of joy.

Torturing to death was far less common among Indians than has been represented in our past propaganda. The preceding examples of the treatment accorded to prisoners indicate the usual custom in such cases. It is probable that if any released prisoner had been captured a second time, after violating his promise that he would not again make war upon his liberators, he would have been subjected to torture, and perhaps tortured to death. Within the framework of Indian concepts of warfare in general, however, there were undoubtedly occasions when a liberated warrior might determine to violate his parole and assume the risk of the penalty he knew would be due to him if he were again captured. If, in such instances, the offender was in fact captured a second time, he habitually bore bravely whatever tortures were inflicted upon him. Indeed, Indian warriors were so strongly motivated by an overpowering desire to exhibit fortitude that they were not entirely disinclined to undergo torture, thus gaining an opportunity to display fortitude to the limit. Under such circumstances, a warrior might hypnotize himself into a state of utter stoicism, in which he was able to defy his tormentors to do their worst.

On the part of the torturers, their actions were conceived as being beneficent rather than punitive or vengeful. The affair was regarded not as an occasion for jubilation, but rather as a time for cleansing the soul. The inflictions were not always carried to the point of death. If it seemed that a lesser degree of cleansing was sufficient—the hardihood of the victim being the prime factor in determining this fact—the natural admiration that he aroused by his conduct usually brought about his release. He was then praised, nursed back to recovery, and often persuaded to become a permanent member of his captors' tribe.

According to the Indian conceptions of warfare, white soldiers did not fight fairly. Whites never engaged in coup touching to demonstrate their bravery, and thus they never afforded their antagonists a chance to resent the insulting touch. They simply began at once to try to kill, and kept on doing nothing else. They did not mourn or show any indication of sorrow at the taking of life. By Indian standards, such opponents may well have seemed to behave like outright murderers rather than like honorable combat opponents. It would therefore seem possible that, under these circumstances, Indian warriors themselves did not feel obliged to show any leniency, and may in fact have consequently modified their behavior.

Contrary to conjectures that have commonly been made, there is no rational ground for a supposition that any Indian in the Custer battle harbored any thought of trying to capture any of the white soldiers for the purpose of torturing them. Doubtless, many of the white men who fought at the Little Bighorn were seriously wounded, and then were heartlessly cut, beaten, and stabbed to death, after which their remains were mangled still further. But, according to Indian ideas, there was no reason for going to the trouble of taking any of these men to the camp, or to any other place, for the purpose of subjecting them to prolonged torture. As the Indians viewed the matter, the whites would not have understood the purpose of such a proceeding. And, perhaps, the Indians may have regarded the white man's soul as at least alien to, if not unworthy of, the cleansing ceremony.

The mode of action according to which the enemy was attacked by Indian warrior societies, or by groups of warriors, in turn has been noted in the narratives of many white men who have participated in Indian battles. Narratives of such incidents as the Wagon Box Fight, the Beecher Island Fight, the Adobe Walls Fight, and similar encounters consistently tell of warriors charging in groups, at different times, and often from different directions. In effect, it is·clear to those who know that the Indian warriors were engaged in practicing a war game among themselves, competing to outdo each other in making coup touches. But practically none of the narrators themselves understood the true meaning of the peculiar Indian maneuvers that they witnessed. Commonly, the Indian movements were attributed to a lack of unity, or to a lack of generalship—as if Indians fought under the command of generals, as our soldiers are accustomed to do.

The Indians surrounding the Custer soldiers undoubtedly

fought in this way. There is proof that this was their style of combat against the Reno men on the hill. Reference may again be made to testimony at the Reno trial. George Herendeen, a scout, testified: "You could not see them. There were probably 500 around him at a time. They didn't use all of their men in a bunch, but in reliefs." Captain Moylan's testimony on this matter runs thus: "I estimate that not less than 900 to 1,000 Indians were in that attack. They relieved each other at intervals, coming from the village." Lieutenant Luther R. Hare estimated the surrounding warriors at 1,000, "although only about 200 at a time were firing." Major Reno was the only one at his trial whose testimony showed some inkling of knowledge of Indian warrior ways in battle. He said: "The Indians are peculiar in their manner of fighting. They don't go in lines or bodies, but in sorties of 5 to 40." In 1929 a full story of the Reno fight, as told by the aged Colonel Varnum, was published in a magazine. In that publication the veteran officer explained that in all battles each Indian warrior fought as an individual, carrying on his fight in his own personal way. It may be, though, that Varnum had learned this during the 53 years since he had been a lieutenant with Reno in 1876, and that he had not known of it at the time.

The general lack of knowledge among whites in general of Indian warrior ways was but little less than that acquired by the white soldiers who fought against them. If the soldiers at Little Bighorn had known enough about Indians and Indian methods of warfare, there need have been no great military disaster there. Indeed, if the knowledge of whites at that time about Indian traits had not been restricted to misleading stories about filth, dog meat, massacre, and torture, there need never have been any battle at Little Bighorn.

WHERE WERE THE INDIANS?

Many writers on the Custer battle have taken the view that the Indians selected their Little Bighorn campsite for the prime purpose of receiving the attack of the soldiers there. This presumption has been connected with a supplementary presumption that plans for an ambush, prepared beforehand, were carried out when the attack was made. Most of the estimates of the length of time that the Indians had been at that spot vary from a few days to a week or so. Some writings indicate that Sitting Bull had chosen the place as a battle ground and had located himself there for some weeks, or longer, before the battle itself occurred. It has been alleged that from this chosen site he sent emissaries to summon or command all other hostile Indians in the entire surrounding wilderness to come and assemble themselves around him. They accordingly did so, and the outcome proved that he was a wonderful military strategist. All of which suppositions are unfounded and ridiculous.

Bands of Plains Indians, even small bands, never stayed long at any one campsite during the summer season. Their prime thought was to follow the buffalo and other game herds. These animals did not linger in large numbers in the immediate vicinity of camps. They moved on, and the Indians moved on after them. Another important consideration was that this was the harvest season for edible roots of various sorts in certain places, as well as the ripening season for various wild fruits and berries at other places. Commonly, such harvesting and gathering times and places had been learned during preceding years. Commonly, too, each Indian band traveled over its same individual route, arriving at approximately the same point on the same seasonal day, from year to year, although changes in route were, of course, sometimes made. Such changes may have been made because of enemies who were stronger or because of economic conditions which invited divergence. Game herds might shift their usual habitat. Richer root and fruit locales might be discovered. But, in the regular course of events, any Indian who had for any reason left his band at a certain campsite would know by counting the elapsed days just where to go to rejoin it again.

The habitual traveling of the Indians in summer was not a picnic or vacation. During the summer the men obtained meat and skins—and stole horses from other tribes. The women dressed the skins, and they stored surplus meat, roots, and fruits for winter use. An ordinary tribal band would not have been satisfied to remain for long at a single campsite beside the Little Bighorn. The great aggregation of tribes could not have found subsistence for themselves there for more than a few days. Another problem was that of subsistence for their ponies, who lived on nothing but natural grass. That great gathering of tribes must have had about 20,000 ponies among them. If all the Indian tribes had indeed been waiting and planning for a long time at that camping spot, all of them, as well as their ponies, would have starved to death before the arrival of the soldiers. Even if the Indians could have stored enough food to support themselves for a week or two at that one place, they could not also have stored food for the ponies. Western plainsmen who know something about the pasturing of horses—especially in the vicinity of that particular camp—can appreciate that it would take only a few days for the ponies to have become so weak as to be useless as war steeds. Seen in this light, the whole conception of a long period of camping at that one site appears ludicrous.

In order to understand where the Indians were during the months preceding the Custer battle, as well as in the two weeks which followed it, we shall trace their movements in detail.

The first bloodshed of the 1876 campaign occurred on March 17. General Crook's soldiers, coming from Fort Fetterman in Wyoming Territory, found an Indian camp on the west side of the Powder River, about ten miles north of the Wyoming line.

He made an early morning surprise attack, chased out the Indians, burned their tipis and their contents, and returned to his base camp at Fort Fetterman. Crook supposed these Indians to be Oglala Sioux, led by Chief Crazy Horse, and his official report designated them as such. Historians, misled by that "official document," thereafter consistently referred to the affray as the destruction of the Crazy Horse village.

But all of the Indians were Northern Cheyenne. There were 40 family lodges of them, and their chief was Old Bear. The author has been acquainted over a period of years with various old Cheyenne who were there. One Cheyenne was killed, two or three wounded. One of those wounded, a man named Braided Locks, still had a bullet-furrow scar along his cheek in his extreme old age.

The Cheyenne band, about 200 of them, fled from the scene. Most of them were on foot, as their pony herd had been cut off by the soldiers. Men, women, and children set off in a northeasterly direction. After three days of travel, they arrived at the camp of Crazy Horse and his Oglala Sioux, where they told what had happened to them. The general impression of both bands was that the whites had declared war only against the Cheyenne. The victims pleaded with the Oglala, their long-time friends and allies, to aid them. News had been received by most of the Indians in the hunting regions that soldiers would come to drive them back to the Dakota reservations. But many of them had doubted the truth of this report. They were in hunting lands acknowledged by treaty as having been set apart for this purpose, and it seemed to them improbable that soldiers would be sent to fight them. But the attack on the Cheyenne camp had proved that they were mistaken.

After two or three days of councilling between the Cheyenne and the Oglala, it was decided that they would go together to a band of Hunkpapa Sioux, led by Chief Sitting Bull, to solicit a triple alliance. The Cheyenne had never been closely associated with the Hunkpapa, but in this case they were willing to ask them for help. The two tribal bands took about three days to make the journey to Sitting Bull's camp. This camp was located near the present-day Eklala, Montana, about 30 miles west of the Dakota western line, which was also the western boundary of the Indian reservation regions.

Sitting Bull and the other Hunkpapa leaders went into council with the Cheyenne and Oglala leaders. Although Sitting Bull was regarded by the United States authorities as an especially hostile Indian, he and his people were somewhat reluctant to engage in any warfare at that time. Instead, they wanted to center their energies upon the usual summer hunting. Finally, however, it was agreed that all three of the bands would travel from place to place together, so that they might more effectively resist any attack by soldiers. It was further agreed that the Cheyenne, being the people who had been attacked and who had solicited the combination, should lead the procession in moving from place to place. The Oglala, closest friends of the Cheyenne, were to follow them. The Hunkpapa were to be last in the column, thus signifying a mere willingness, rather than a positive desire, to engage in whatever warfare might ensue.

Early in April the three bands started out in the agreed upon order. They moved in short marches so that their ponies might graze along the way on the new grass just beginning to come up. Their course was directed northwestward down an eastern tributary of the Powder River until they reached the main stream 30 or 35 miles above its mouth. There they turned westward to go to the Tongue River. Other Indians belonging to the three tribes had joined them along the way, as also had bands of Minneconjou Sioux, Blackfeet Sioux, and Sans Arcs Sioux. Thus, altogether six different tribal bands were represented.

In traveling, the Cheyenne continued to lead, while the Hunkpapa continued to bring up the rear. The other four tribes were in their separate groups between the leaders and the rear guard. Six separate tribal camp circles were set up at each camping place. The Cheyenne circle was placed at the forward position, in the direction of movement, and the Hunkpapa circle was placed at the rearmost position. The other four tribal camp circles were placed at points in between.

The Indian bands continued westward to Rosebud Creek, or River. They arrived there about May 19. This date is fixed by computation of the time their camps were seen there by scouts from the Gibbon contingent of soldiers, then on the north side of the Yellowstone River. Other precise dates concerning Indian campings have been fixed upon in a similar way. Of course, Indians in those times knew nothing of our calendar system. But a joint study carried out by the veterans among them in association with the author has enabled precise or approximate dates to be established for all their campings during that time. The veterans remembered each place of camping, and they remembered exactly or approximately how long they stayed at each place, why they stayed or did not stay, and where they were when specially notable incidents took place. The author, for his part, knows precise dates for many such notable incidents, having learned the dates from soldiers' diaries or other writings. It has been easy, then, to connect the links and make a map of Indian travels, with dates of encampment at all of the places having historic importance.

Because the Indians were hunting buffalo and grazing their ponies en route, the rate of travel was slow. It took them about six weeks to go from the Hunkpapa Sioux camp east of Powder River to the first camping place on the Rosebud, a distance of about 150 miles. At some places the stops were for one-night stands. At others, where great buffalo herds invited them or where the women needed to tan skins or gather roots, the stops were of longer duration. At other times the moves were merely for a mile or so, to give the ponies good grazing.

The first encampment on the Rosebud was about eight miles above its mouth. The last encampment on that stream took the form of an array of camp circles centered on what is now the Busby post office, on the present Northern Cheyenne Reservation. Incidentally, the Cheyenne still preserve untouched by any plow the entire area on which their own camp circle was placed near Busby. Furthermore, on two or three occasions in recent years, that particular area has been the scene of tribal Sun Dance ceremonies. These Sun Dance ceremonies have been held each time on dates which included June 25, the anniversary date of the Custer battle.

The combined tribes left the Rosebud on the morning of June 15, to go to the Little Bighorn Valley. That night they made what they term a "dry camp"—one with no stream of water nearby—just east of the divide between the Rosebud and the Little Bighorn. This site, as pointed out to the author by the old Cheyenne warriors, is on an extreme upper tributary of Tullock Creek. On the next day, June 16, they went on over the divide and down a stream that is now named Reno Creek. At the forks of this creek, almost ten miles by air from the present Custer Battlefield National Monument, the camps were set up for the night.

Soldiers had been seen to the southward, somewhere near what is now Sheridan, Wyoming, while the Indians were encamped at the Busby site. It appears that this news was a factor in causing them to turn westward to the Little Bighorn instead of going on southward up the Rosebud. At all times, the plans of their chiefs were to evade the soldiers if they could do so. The

chiefs did not consider their own aggregated peoples as constituting a war party seeking a fight. They had their families and
all of their home properties with them. Indeed, the situation as
they saw it was that they were at home all of the time during
their travels. Many eager young warriors were, of course, more
than willing to go out and perform brave deeds of resistance.
But the chiefs and old men, with the women backing them,
urged a continued strict observance of the usual hunting life.
Their view was that if all of the Indians could go through the
entire summer without seeing any white soldiers, they would
consider that they had done well.

But reports came that the soldiers seen to the southward were
coming toward the Indians. The young warriors clamored to go
out to meet them, to keep them away from the home tipis. With
the encouragement of some of the chiefs, who accompanied them,
hundreds of warriors from all of the camp circles rode away up
South Reno Creek on the night of June 16 in search of the soldiers. The next morning they found them far up Rosebud Creek.
A battle ensued which lasted several hours. Nine soldiers and
several more Indians were killed. Late in the afternoon the soldiers retreated and the Indians left the field to return to their
camp. The soldiers were led by General Crook, and the battle
became known in historical writings as Crook's Battle of the
Rosebud, which took place on June 17, eight days before the
Custer battle. The Indians, for their part, however, neither knew
nor cared who was the leader of the white soldiers.

Mistakes as to the identity of the Indians and as to the location
of their camp were made by Crook and his followers at the
battle. These mistakes were accepted as true data at the time,
and they have been repeated in writings since then. The Indian
opponents were said to be "Crazy Horse and his Oglalas," and
their camp was said to have been down the Rosebud and a few
miles below the battle site. During the course of the conflict a
detachment of troops was sent in that direction to attack the
supposed camp, but as they approached a canyon where Indians
might be lying in ambush, Crook recalled them.

A mistaken confirmation of the supposition that the Indian
camp was just a few miles below the battle ground was made
later on. In order to understand how the mistaken confirmation
came about it is necessary to jump forward about two weeks in
time in tracing the Indians' movements, and then to make another
jump forward of about seven weeks in considering Crook's
operations.

After the Custer battle, the Indians moved about 35 miles up the Little Bighorn Valley, then went east over a divide to the uppermost Rosebud Creek, then continued on down that stream, and finally moved eastward until they disbanded. During the early part of that retreat, on the night of June 29, they camped on an extreme western tip of the Rosebud, several miles west of the Crook battle site. The next day, June 30, they passed down over that battle ground, went on through the canyon, and set their camp for that night not far below it. They left the next day to continue their journey away from the region.

Early in August, Crook returned in search of troublesome Indians. His return was over the same route he had followed in June. He and his soldiers stopped to examine their battlefield. As they marched on down the Rosebud they found, just below the canyon, the vacated campsite of the Indians. They had no knowledge of the Indians' having been there on June 30, so it was quite natural for them to consider that this was the campsite of the Indians at the time of the battle on June 17. Their error is excusable, for it is only in recent times that the details of the movements that the Indians made then have become known. Using information not available to Crook and his men, it is now easy to see that the warriors who fought them on June 17 were from all of the tribes, and that their camp was then at the forks of Reno Creek, about 25 miles from where the fighting took place.

The day after the Rosebud battle, the Indians moved down to the Little Bighorn. Their camp circles were set up at spots about a mile and a half to three miles above the mouth of Reno Creek and on the east side of the Little Bighorn. The Cheyenne camp was at the upper southern end of the array, while the Hunkpapa Sioux camp was at the lower northern end. Since the Cheyenne were still leading and the Hunkpapa were still last in both traveling and camping, their locations at that camping place show an intention to go southward up the Little Bighorn Valley.

Great herds of buffalo were found on the hills west of this camp, just above the mouth of Reno Creek. It was the night of June 18, and the adjacent grazing lands used by the ponies were at their richest. In order to make general forays into the buffalo herds, the council of chiefs decided to stay there for a while. They stayed six nights, until June 24. Meantime, vast herds of antelope had been seen west of the Bighorn River. As the women wanted antelope skins just then, the previous plan to go up the

Little Bighorn Valley was changed. Instead, it was decided to go down the valley to its junction with the Bighorn, about 20 miles northward. From the camps set up there, the hunters would cross to the west side of the Bighorn and get among the antelope herds.

The Cheyenne doubled back past the other camp circles, and set off northward down the Little Bighorn. The Oglala dropped in behind them, the other tribes followed, and the Hunkpapa again took their regular place at the rear. They crossed the Little Bighorn and traveled down its west side. After a short journey of four or five miles, they set up camp for the night of June 24. They expected to make another short move the next day, and yet another on the following day, which would have taken them to the mouth of the Little Bighorn.

Their statements that they had intended to stay only one night at that June 24 camping place are supported by a consideration of the conditions then existing. At the preceding location they had obtained a big supply of buffalo meat and skins, which kept them so occupied that they stayed there for six nights. Then, needing antelope meat and skins, they decided to go to the mouth of the Little Bighorn and to use it as a base for antelope hunting. They had nothing else in prospect until they reached that base, so there was no reason, as far as they then knew, for them to stop more than one night at any place along the way.

The fact that the soldiers found them still encamped at or after the middle of the day on June 25 is not strong proof that they had planned to stay there another night. Indians not urged by necessity often moved only a few miles, perhaps taking only an hour or so to make a move which they called a day's work. They had traveled four or five miles on June 24. The remaining distance to the mouth of the Little Bighorn was 12 to 14 miles. They did not need to start early on either of the two additional days contemplated for the remainder of the journey. The Indians say that a considerable number of tipis had been taken down, in preparation for the move, when the soldiers came. Accounts by soldiers also say that when they arrived, some tipis were already down, while packs were being made ready to leave the camp. But the soldiers attributed these preparations solely to their approach and to an intention to flee from them.

There is strong circumstantial support for Indian statements that their contemplated course at that time was northward down the valley. In the camp where the soldiers found them, the Hunkpapa were near the present Garryowen railroad station, at the encampment's south end—the direction from which the tribes had just come. The Cheyenne were at the encampment's north end—the direction in which the tribes were expecting to go. Moreover, the Cheyenne and Hunkpapa had had these foremost and rearmost positions respectively at every camping place where they had stopped for almost three months.

It is also believable that the Indians were surprised, as they say they were, at the arrival of the soldiers. This is indicated by the circumstances prevailing when the first charge was made by the soldiers. Practically all of the tipis were standing. A great throng of women, children, and old people left the camp and went running away from the soldiers to the hills. The troops were quite close to the camps before they met resistance. The warriors meeting them were only a few when compared with the great numbers who came afterward. The first few were probably mostly the camp policemen, or dog soldiers, which every Indian tribal camp regularly kept ready for immediate action. The many who came afterward were all the other warriors. They were not at first ready, since they had not known that they would be needed.

If the approach of the soldiers had been known a sufficient time beforehand, the situation at the camp would have been quite different from what it actually was. All of the tipis would have been down. All of the household property would have been in packs, and the packs would have been on the pack ponies. Everything would have been ready to be taken away with the women, children, and old people, instead of being abandoned, as was the actual case. Or, if the warning had been given in time to allow even some part of such preparations to be made, that same extra time would have allowed the warriors—and many more of them—to have prepared themselves and advanced further out from the camps than they did. In this way they would have shielded their families in the camps and given them time to escape, even though the necessity of flight might not have been seen as pressing, but rather as a matter to be determined by events.

In the event, it seems a reasonable estimate that 15 to 20 minutes elapsed between the time when the first Indian learned of the impending attack and the time when the attack occurred. It is probable that the first observer was a Hunkpapa, since theirs was the camp approached by Reno. The other camps were strung out for two miles northward. Some minutes would elapse before word could be spread to all of them. In fact, a large number of the people in the camps first got notice of the attack when they heard the shooting of the guns just south of the Hunkpapa camp.

There was a whirlwind of excitement and bewilderment in all the camps. Pony herds were hurried in for warriors to get their mounts. There was a rushing to get ready, and a rushing forth by each warrior as soon as he was prepared. Family noncombatants seized packs and ran for the hills. Many ran without packs, abandoning all property. Frail old people shuffled along. Sick people made off as best they could. Children screamed for mothers not in sight. Distracted mothers tried to find children lost in the tempestuous melee.

A selected campsite and a cunning ambush to entrap Custer? What a ridiculous fancy!

The noncombatants remained on the western hills and watched the progress of the fighting from afar. When it became evident that their warriors had won the contest, there was a general return to the camps. But all of the tipis were then taken down and all the camps were moved to adjacent locations to the northwest. The shift was made on account of the deaths of warriors from the different tribes. This was the established Indian custom —to move camp at once when a death occurred. The noncombatants stayed at the second campsite that night and until late in the afternoon of the next day, while the warriors fought the Reno men entrenched on their hill. Then the whole aggregation of tribes started to move southward up the Little Bighorn Valley.

THE CHARGES AGAINST CUSTER

General Custer has been charged—and often bitterly charged—with having been the sole cause of his annihilating defeat. It has been charged that he rushed his march in order to get at the Indians first and thus obtain all the glory for himself. Extensive arguments have been advanced for and against the question of whether he disobeyed General Terry's orders; or, if he did, if he was justified in doing so. It has been maintained that he maliciously sent Major Reno into a hopeless charge. It has been contended that he intentionally sent Captain Benteen to one side for the purpose of keeping this capable officer out of the fight. All of this has been alleged to have been done so that none but Custer would receive the praise.

Let us review the pertinent points in the case.

The march up the Rosebud Valley, between noon on June 22 and the late afternoon of June 24, was not a hurried one, as compared with many other similar movements his troops or other cavalry units had made. Although it was generally believed that the Indians were on the Little Bighorn, for all that anyone knew they might have been 50 or more miles up that stream from where they were actually found, or else they might have moved from the Little Bighorn to another valley. The uncertainty which prevailed is shown by the fact that the Seventh Cavalry, as it was about to go after the Indians, was rationed for 15 days. Aware of this uncertainty. Custer planned not to hurry at first. Evidence of such a plan may be found in Lieutenant Wallace's diary, in an entry dated June 23: "General Custer stated that for the first few days short marches would be made, and then increased."

The Seventh Cavalry traveled about 12 miles up the Rosebud during the afternoon of June 22. The next day, the 23rd, the distance covered was about 32 miles, with the troops camping at about 5 P.M. On the 24th it was 28 miles, with camp being made at the site just below the present Busby school. Here Custer learned for certain that the Indians had turned west to go over the divide to the Little Bighorn. After some hours of rest, he decided to follow the trail by making a night march. This was done, and when dawn came on the 25th he was near the top of the divide, having moved about 12 miles during the night.

In the Terry-Custer march from Dakota, when the troops had wagons, a beef herd, and infantry with them, Godfrey mentioned daily distances covered as being from 10 to 40 miles. The diary of Mark Kellogg, a newspaper man, tells of their traveling 32 miles on June 7, but he comments on that distance as being specially remarkable, since at that time the route was over badlands country east of the lower Powder River.

Custer often made rapid marches, and so did other cavalry leaders. His account of his operations on the southern Plains in the late 1860s includes this: "Our average daily march, when not in pursuit of the enemy, was about 25 miles." He moved faster, of course, on special occasions. On the Yellowstone, in 1873, when he had a wagon train with him and was not following any Indians, he marched 32 miles in one day. During his Black Hills expedition, in 1874, he wrote to his wife of having marched 45 miles in one day, and this was at a time when no pursuit was being made.

General Wesley Merritt, in 1879, led a battalion of the Fifth Cavalry 170 miles between 11 A.M. on October 2 and 5:30 P.M. on October 5—less than four days—at an average pace of about 45 miles per day He also had a battalion of infantry in wagons with him, and he grumbled about their impeding his march. His soldiers were hastening to head off some Indians reported on the rampage in South Dakota. In July 1876, when a band of Indians was about to leave Pine Ridge Reservation to join the Sitting Bull hostiles, Merritt and his Fifth Cavalry went after them at the rate of 75 miles in 35 hours. During the 1879 troubles, Captain F. S. Dodge marched his command 80 miles in 16 hours, and Lieutenant Wood led one troop of the Fourth Cavalry 70 miles in 12 hours.

General Gibbon's soldiers, with General Terry accompanying them, left the mouth of the Rosebud at the same time that Custer departed from that point. The Gibbon forces traveled up the Yellowstone, the Bighorn, and the Little Bighorn. Their rate of movement was about the same as that of Custer during those same days. Lieutenant Bradley's diary reveals that they were moving as fast as they could. He notes complaints that his 12 mounted infantrymen were very tired, as he was himself. The four troops of cavalry with Gibbon made a night march in order to reach the mouth of the Little Bighorn about midnight of June 25. Lieutenant McClernand, of the Gibbon infantry, records in his diary that his men walked almost 53 miles on June 25 and 26.

Daily rates of military march on the western Plains were, however, governed by many factors. Besides the condition of the route, there was the important matter of camping where water, fuel, and grass were available.

The usual estimates of Custer's double march on the night of June 24 and the forenoon of June 25 appear too high in mileage. The total distance of those closely successive moves has been mentioned in figures varying from 35 to 40 or more miles. But the present-day road from the campsite he left, a mile north of the present Busby post office, to the nearest edge of the Indian camps, adjacent to the present Garryowen railroad station, runs about 27 miles. Busby post office is due east from Garryowen, and the distance between these two points is exactly 23 miles. So it seems that the total of Custer's doubleheader march may reasonably be estimated at about 26 miles, unless he wandered considerably from his natural route.

Terry offered to let Custer take up the Rosebud with him the three Gatling guns they had brought from Dakota. Custer declined the offer, saying that since the guns were drawn by condemned cavalry horses and since there was much rough country to be traversed, they could not keep up with his pack mules, much less keep up with his men mounted on good horses. Therefore, if he took them, his march would be slowed down considerably. This refusal has been construed as stemming from Custer's desire to strip down for winning the race to reach the

Indians. But Terry, the superior officer, could have ordered him to take them. The fact that such order was not made indicates that he was willing to let Custer move as fast as he could.

Another offer was a proposal that four troops of the Second Cavalry be sent with the Custer forces. These were under the immediate command of Major James S. Brisbin and were a part of the forces of General Gibbon, located in his camp just across the Yellowstone north from the mouth of the Rosebud. The idea of sending them with Custer appears to have originated with Brisbin. He mentioned it to Gibbon, and Gibbon mentioned it to Terry. Terry, the highest ranking officer, asked Custer what he thought about it.

Custer expressed a belief that his own full regiment of 12 troops of cavalry could deal successfully with whatever situation might arise. This was in fact a natural and reasonable reaction, rather than one deserving criticism. If Brisbin and his men were under the command of Custer, the situation would be strange both to them and to him, and several days would be needed to achieve smooth cooperation. Even if Terry had accompanied them as the supreme commander, the adjustments might have taken too long in a situation in which rapid shifts might be necessary. Furthermore, the detaching of the four cavalry troops from Gibbon—especially if Terry had accompanied them—would have left him with only five companies of infantry. Terry must have thought of all this, for he could have made the transfer without asking Custer. Nevertheless, the refusal of the offer of the Brisbin cavalrymen has been cited as evidence which showed that Custer harbored a theatrical determination to be the sole hero of the campaign.

A change in Custer's usual mood is said to have come over him during the march up the Rosebud. Godfrey and other officers then with him say that his usual snappiness or sarcasm was greatly subdued. They also say that his manner was serious and meditative, and that he engaged in an unusual man-to-man conferring with his subordinate officers. His critics have taken this as signifying something to his discredit. Some express the opinion that he was brooding over his troubles with superiors in Washington, including President Grant, and that his mind was deeply absorbed in devising schemes to achieve a glorious victory that would overcome these troubles. Others offer the theory that he had a guilty conscience on account of his having determined to ignore all of Terry's orders or suggestions as to his course on this march.

But there was another matter just then that might have worried or, at least, perplexed him. This was the question as to the number of Indians whose trail he was following, as well as to exactly where they might be found. Godfrey and others tell of the many Indian camping places they encountered on June 23 and 24. At various places the moves made by the Indians appeared to have been very short ones, consisting of several shiftings in close succession. An estimate was made that there were 380 lodges, the number of Indians in them being about 1,500. At many places the number of lodges appeared less, but in such instances it was supposed that the whole number of tipis had not been set up.

A reference to the preceding chapter outlining the movements of the combined tribes will clarify this mistaken conclusion as to how many Indians were traveling together. There were six separate tribal bands, and they made their six separate camp circles close to each other at the various campsites. The pursuers did not know this. They supposed that only one camp circle made the marks they saw. Forty-five years afterwards, in 1921, General Godfrey confessed this to be a mistake. Discussing the matter in a Montana Historical Society publication, he pointed out the significant features that they should have observed in 1876, but had overlooked.

The army men in the field had been misinformed by reports from Washington. These reports were, of course, based on Indian Office information received from local agents on the Dakota reservations. The agents declared that they had only a few absentees. Such false representations appear to have had a corrupt foundation. In those times the Indians were receiving some treaty payments as well as liberal quantities of rations and other gifts, all distributed through the agents. These government allocations were made according to a per capita count on each reservation. Every agent, therefore, had the constant incentive to claim the continual presence of all the Indians—and more— who belonged on the reservation under his control. Rations and gifts were then sent to be apportioned among them. If the agent reported absentees, he afterwards had to report what disposal he had made of the allowances forfeited by such absentees. If the agent could hide the fact of any absences, it would appear "on paper" that all were present and had received their gifts or payments due. Then all of the absentees' gifts or payments could be diverted to the control or account of the agent. Washington was, therefore, regularly told that all of the Indians were at home.

But Custer had with him some helpers who knew nothing about official reports from Washington. These were about 30 Arikara Indian scouts, 6 Crow Indian scouts, and 1 half-Sioux, Mitch Buoyer, who acted as his guide. The Crow Indians and Mitch Buoyer knew the Rosebud and Little Bighorn and contiguous regions thoroughly, and they also knew thoroughly the habitual summer journeyings of the Cheyenne and Sioux through these regions. It was not difficult for any one of them to combine this knowledge with an observation of the campsites and thereby to conclude that there was a great aggregation of different tribes traveling together.

Maybe they told Custer, or maybe they did not. Old-time Indians were often not insistently communicative in such situations. It is probable that they supposed he already knew, and knew much more than they did. To their way of thinking, he could not help but know, since the evidence was as plainly in view as the river and the hills. Or, if any one of them did make known his judgment as to the number of Indians, he might have been discouraged from making further revelations. Mitch Buoyer is reported to have offered the opinion that if those Indians were encountered there was going to be "a hell of a big fight" and that it might last more than one day. Custer is said to have made a withering reply to the scout in which he ridiculed this opinion.

On the other hand, it is also possible that the scouts told Custer about their deductions as to the number of Indians, or else that he absorbed their conclusions from their actions as well as from their casual communications. He may have been convinced by them, but decided it was best to keep the matter to himself. It may have been that in the frequent conferences with his officers—remarked on by them as a departure from his usual pattern of behavior—he was hoping that one or more of them would spontaneously announce a belief that they were following a very large body of Indians, and thus help him to settle whatever doubts he might have. On the question of the number of Indians alone, he had enough food for thought to transform him into a serious and meditative man.

The departure of the Custer column from the Rosebud to go over the divide toward the Little Bighorn is the major action he took which resulted in his being charged with having disobeyed Terry's orders. In fact, the entire communication as written by Terry took the form of suggestions, not of outright commands. Terry expressed the opinion that if the Indian trail should be found to lead from the Rosebud over to the Little Bighorn, it would be best for Custer to keep on going up the Rosebud and on southward to the headwaters of the Tongue River. This was so that, while Gibbon and his men would be going up the Bighorn and the Little Bighorn, the Indians could not escape from him by the upper Tongue River route. There was, however, an expressed disavowal of intent to bind Custer, and a declaration of confidence in his using his own discretion. Notwithstanding this, his keeping on the trail as it turned westward from the Rosebud has been held against Custer as a violation of orders and as evidence showing that he was actuated solely by personal ambition.

There was another highly pertinent clause in the Terry order— or the Terry instructions, as the paper in question is more often designated. This is the reference to the Gibbon troops moving up the Yellowstone and the Bighorn to the mouth of the Little Bighorn. Terry was to accompany them, not in immediate command, but as commander of the entire department. An appointment for a meeting with Custer at the mouth of the Little Bighorn is put in these words: "And the department commander desires that you report to him there not later than the expiration of the time for which your troops are rationed, unless in the meantime you receive further orders."

The Custer troops were rationed for 15 days as to hardtack, coffee, and sugar, and for 12 days as to bacon. The rationing was on June 22. So the latest date at which he was to arrive at the mouth of the Little Bighorn might have been construed as either July 4 or July 7. It was also of course allowable for him to arrive there on any day before then. But the estimate was made that the Gibbon forces would arrive at the mouth of the Little Bighorn on June 26. As it developed, their cavalrymen—the four troops under Brisbin—arrived there about midnight on the 25th, while their infantrymen arrived early in the forenoon of the 26th. It has been consistently contended since then that the 26th was the junction date specially mentioned or urged in all of the conferences in which Terry, Gibbon, Custer, and others participated at the mouth of the Rosebud. But sticking precisely to the 26th is incompatible with Custer's rationing for 12 to 15 days.

Let us suppose that Custer had quit the Indian trail and gone on southward up the Rosebud, as the Terry instructions suggested. Being in camp at Busby for the night of the 24th, the next day of travel at the rate he had been going would have ended in his camping in the vicinity of present-day Ranchester, Wyoming, on the Tongue River. On the 26th he would have had to travel about 30 miles northwestward in order to reach the present Wyola, Montana, on the upper Little Bighorn River, about 50 miles above its mouth. It would have required two more days, the 27th and 28th, for him to have arrived at the mouth of the Little Bighorn to make the junction with Gibbon which it has been claimed he was expected to make on the 26th. To one who knows the local geography, it is easy to understand that it would have been utterly impossible for Custer to follow on up the Rosebud and also to be at the mouth of the Little Bighorn on the 26th. It is altogether probable that as he pondered over the paper during his march up the Rosebud he saw the incompatibility of the two suggestions.

Where, however, were the Indians going to be during that time? It appears that none of the critics has given any thought to this factor in the case. As we saw earlier, the Indians first arrived on the Little Bighorn on the afternoon of June 18. They set up their six camp circles five or six miles up the river from the present Garryowen railroad station. On the 24th they started for the mouth of the Little Bighorn, traveling five or six miles and making camp just below the present Garryowen. The next morning the Custer soldiers struck them, the terrific battle ensued, and the Indian plans were changed. But their intention had been to move on a short distance down the Little Bighorn on the 25th, and to continue their march on the 26th. At their slow rate of movement this would have brought them to the river junction on the afternoon of the 26th.

The Gibbon forces—cavalry and infantry, with Terry accompanying them—left the mouth of the Little Bighorn at about 9 A.M. on June 26 and set out to go up the Little Bighorn. At this time the Indians, if they had not been fighting Custer, would have been about ready to start on their final few miles of travel to the mouth of the Little Bighorn. So Gibbon would have met them two or three miles above the mouth of that stream, unless the discovery of each other's presence had been made on the morning of the 26th.

Where would Custer have been? We have already mentioned the estimate that on the morning of the 26th he would have been a few miles northwest of the present Ranchester, Wyoming, and about 60 miles south of this assumed encounter between Gibbon and the Indians.

What would have been the outcome of a battle between the Gibbon forces and the Indians? He had a total of about 450 men, while Custer had almost 700. But practically every man with

Gibbon was a veteran, while Custer had a large percentage of fresh recruits. There is plenty of room for conjecture as to the result of a battle between Gibbon and the Indians. If the soldiers had won, Custer would doubtless have felt that he had been tricked out of honors. If the soldiers had lost, there would probably have been wrangling as to who was at fault, for faultfinding is easy mental work.

Another complexity may be noted here. If Custer had gone on up the Rosebud, during the first day of travel after leaving the Busby camp he would have reached a place where soldiers and Indians had been in a big battle. The Indians had met General Crook there on June 17 and had driven him back into Wyoming. What effect this discovery would have had on Custer is an insoluble problem. But news of the Crook fight had not reached Terry, Gibbon, Custer, or anybody else in their region. So it was not considered in the Terry instructions, and it could not have been in Custer's thoughts at the time he was deciding his course.

The impossibility of Custer's being at the mouth of the Little Bighorn on the 26th if he kept going up the Rosebud placed upon him the necessity of deciding which of Terry's two contradictory suggestions he ought to adopt. This was another matter to ponder over which could have explained his serious and meditative mood. His decision was not announced until some hours after they had reached the Busby camp. Then, after darkness had fallen, he assembled his officers and told them he would leave the Rosebud and follow the Indian trail toward the Little Bighorn. This was on the night of the 24th. He said that that night he would go only far enough to make observations from high points the next morning, and that no attack would be made before the 26th. This move would also have been the right one to make to enable him to arrive at the mouth of the Little Bighorn on the 26th, if no Indians had been encountered. This was in conformity with this aspect of the Terry instructions.

The night march was made. At dawn the regiment went into bivouac camp in a gulch just east of the divide—the location chosen for concealment. Custer went far forward with some of his scouts to look out from high points toward the Little Bighorn Valley. The scouts declared they could see smoke from an Indian camp at a certain place in the valley. Custer expressed disbelief in the accuracy of their observations, but it appears he finally decided to accept their judgment. As he was returning to the temporary camp, and was almost there, he saw the column of soldiers coming over the divide. He uttered an exclamation of astonishment and irritation on account of this movement, and he began to make inquiries as to who had ordered it. He became composed, however, when a full explanation was made. During his absence on the forward scouting trip, an unexpected incident of great importance had occurred.

Some of the packed property had been lost from the mules during the march of the preceding night. The loss included a box of hardtack and a bag of clothing belonging to Sergeant Curtis of the quartermaster corps. Curtis took a few men with him and went back on the trail to search for the lost articles. They found them, and they also found two or three Indians rummaging in the box and the bag. Curtis fired upon the Indians, and they fled. When he returned to the command, he reported what had occurred. It appeared evident, in consequence of this Indian contact, that concealment was no longer possible, and that all of the hostile Indians would soon know of the presence of the soldiers.

This was a very important incident—indeed, the key incident that not only changed Custer's plan but also changed the whole course of events in the 1876 campaign. The upset in plans was caused, however, by a misconception of the true character of the incident. What happened was as follows. Little Wolf, a Cheyenne chief, was leading seven lodges of his people from South Dakota to join the hostiles. During the day of June 24, on the Rosebud, his band discovered the trail of the cavalrymen following the trail of the Indians. They saw the Custer men go into camp at Busby, saw them leave there at night, and watched them from the rear the next morning. The Little Wolf people were frightened, but although some of them wanted to turn back to South Dakota, they kept on dodging from ridge to ridge behind the soldiers. They found the lost bundles and were then shot at by Sergeant Curtis. They remained in the rear of the soldiers and did not go to the camps until after the Custer fight had ended.

The following of Custer by the Little Wolf band appears to be the false basis for a persisting supposition that Custer's approach was known to all of the hostiles a day or so before his arrival, and that they were fully prepared to receive him. In fact, the earliest knowledge any of the Indians in the camps had of the presence of the soldiers was only a quarter of an hour, or perhaps a little more, before the Reno men made their first charge.

Many of the Indians got their first notice of the attack when they heard the firing of the guns.

The plan Custer announced to his officers when he told them he would leave the Rosebud was similar to the plans he had carried out on two preceding occasions in his Indian campaigns. The first occasion was in April 1867, and the action taken was the first military move ever made by the Seventh Cavalry, just then organized. It was decided to capture a band of Cheyenne on Pawnee Fork, just north of Fort Larned, Kansas. General Hancock, as Custer's superior officer, was in command. The Cheyenne camp was surrounded during the night. It was the intention of the cavalry to demand a surrender the next morning. But the Indians learned of what was happening, and all of them slipped away during the night, leaving their tipis standing.

The other occasion was at the Washita, in November 1868. Custer, as the highest ranking officer present, and not Hancock, was leading the regiment. The Washita instance also differed from Pawnee Fork by virtue of the fact that Custer did not plan to capture the Indians but to fight them. He first tentatively located the Cheyenne camp on November 26. That same night he located it precisely and placed his soldiers to surround it. At dawn the next morning he made an attack from all sides. The result was a smashing victory for Custer.

It seems plainly evident that, in the case of the Little Bighorn, the Washita plan was contemplated. The soldiers and the horses were to rest all day on the 25th, while observations were to be made. Having located the camp—although whether there was any camp in that vicinity he did not yet know—he would place his men around it during the night of the 25th, and at dawn of the 26th the attack would be made. He knew that he had many green soldiers. He knew that they were tired and that the horses were tired on that morning of the 25th, and that all would be more tired if they kept on going forward just then. If he had thoughts of getting in ahead of Gibbon, he knew it was not necessary for him to attack on the 25th, for Gibbon would not arrive at the mouth of the Little Bighorn until the 26th. Thus, Gibbon's soldiers at that time would still be about 15 miles from the Indian camp which the scouts said they had located. As it developed later, the Gibbon soldiers actually arrived at the present Crow Agency, two or three miles below the Indian campsites, just at sunset on June 26.

Why, then, hasten to the attack on the 25th instead of waiting until the early morning of the 26th? Rational and unbiased thought can attribute to Custer in this regard only one incentive— a fear that otherwise the Indians would escape and leave him holding an empty bag. This was a prime consideration in all military circles during the campaign. There was no talk or any apparent expectation of defeat in battle. The main problem discussed was rather how to catch the Indians and compel them to fight. All the officers in all the military bodies in the field were in constant trepidation lest the elusive red people should escape.

Some ground for censure of Custer exists in his not complying with Terry's request to send a courier with a message down Tullock Creek to inform Terry of any developments during the Rosebud march. The Busby camp might have been an appropriate point of departure for such a courier, but the bivouac camp just east of the divide would appear a more fitting point. This early morning pause of the 25th took place at the extreme upper tributaries of Tullock Creek. On that day, according to the schedule, the Terry-Gibbon soldiers would be traveling along the hills bordering the lower part of the creek on their way toward the mouth of the Little Bighorn.

But up to Sunday morning Custer had no new information to send Terry. It already had been the theory that the Indians had left the Rosebud to go to the Little Bighorn. The only news he could have sent would have been after he had returned from his early morning scouting. Perhaps he intended to send word that his Indian scouts had seen a camp in the valley, but the supposed discovery of him by the hostiles and his decision to proceed to attack made it seem better for him to await the outcome of the attack. There was still no opportunity for him to know whether the camp seen was a small one or a large one, and whether the Indians were all together or were scattered along the valley. In the event, the omission to send a courier to Terry did no harm. It merely created another item to be pointed to by Custer's critics showing that he was too eager to occupy the center of the stage. Yet, how the sending of a courier to Terry just then would have hindered Custer's aspirations is not clear. His sending a message would not have stopped him—and ought not to have stopped him —from the course he had decided upon.

Terry had joined Sheridan in urging that Custer be released from his detention at Washington, despite his disfavor with the War Department and the Indian Office. He had urged that he be sent back at once to his regiment in order to lead his men in the campaign. Confidence in him was specifically expressed in Terry's

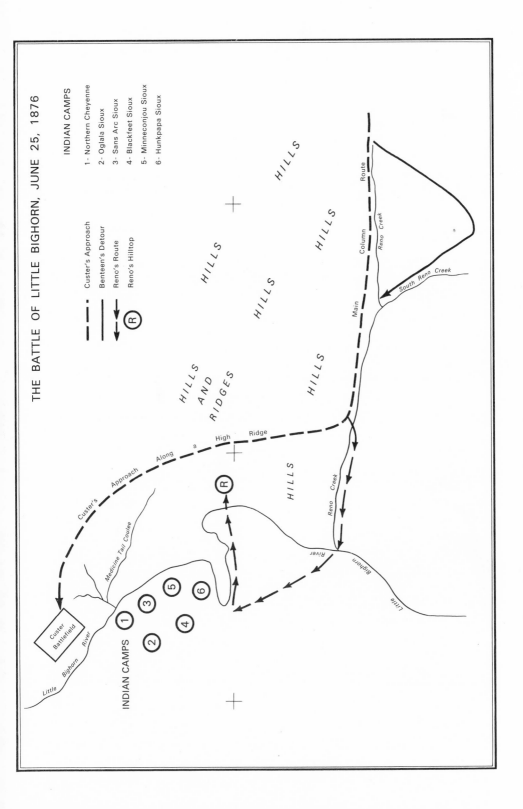

THE BATTLE OF LITTLE BIGHORN, JUNE 25, 1876

INDIAN CAMPS

1 - Northern Cheyenne
2 - Oglala Sioux
3 - Sans Arc Sioux
4 - Blackfeet Sioux
5 - Minneconjou Sioux
6 - Hunkpapa Sioux

Custer's Approach
Benteen's Detour
Reno's Route
Reno's Hilltop

instructions at the time of their final parting. The offer of the Gatling guns and the offer of the four troops of Second Cavalry led by Brisbin may be construed as not only an indication of confidence in Custer but also as an indication that it was expected of him that he would do the main part of the fighting.

Some of Terry's spoken words have been quoted as showing that he feared that Custer would be too reckless. But if he really entertained such a fear, his offers of more troops could have been reversed, and Custer's strength reduced by detaching some of the Seventh Cavalry troops and assigning them to Brisbin and Gibbon. This would have been the most effective way to curb Custer, and Terry had full authority to do so if he had so desired. It is probable that Terry was worried to some extent by thoughts of what Custer might do, or might try to do. But it also is probable that such worrying was based not on any distrust of Custer himself, but on concern about the large number of inexperienced soldiers in his ranks.

The dividing of Custer's forces at the last moment before proceeding to the attack has been condemned by practically all reviewers of this action. But the condemnations have been based on knowledge gained afterwards, whereas judgment should be rendered on the basis of the knowledge available to Custer at that time. There were important conditions he did not know, and was not afforded an opportunity to know. This was because the supposed discovery of his presence had prevented his spending the day of the 25th in making observations, and it had led him to decide to attack at once. We have already considered some of the important conditions not known to Custer in the preceding chapter detailing the movements of the Indians.

From their camp at the forks of what we know as Reno Creek, about ten miles southeast from the Custer battlefield, the Indian warriors went southeastward up South Reno Creek and fought General Crook's soldiers through the day of June 17. At the end of that day, they returned by the same route. The many hundreds of ponies which went out and returned made a heavy trail along the stream. The Indian scouts with Custer, and possibly Custer himself, saw the trail when they made their early morning observations. Custer did not know there had been a battle with Crook, so it was reasonable for him to suppose that the South Reno Creek trail had been made by some Indians encamped in that direction.

Captain Benteen—with Troops H, D, and K—was sent over the hills toward South Reno Creek, while the main column continued

on the trail they had been following, which now led down central Reno Creek. Benteen was merely given a terse order: "Pitch
into anything you come across." He and his men did much riding
over rough hills, but they found no indication of Indians there.
They therefore returned to the original trail and fell in just ahead
of the mule pack train that was lagging some miles behind the
main column. Benteen's return took place just above the forks
of the creek, so it appears he never saw the South Reno Creek
trail.

Benteen and all other reviewers of Custer's act in sending him
to one side have professed mystification as to the reason for it.
But Custer's omission of any explanation as to why he sent Benteen in that direction does not provide ground for censure of him.
In the first place, he may have wanted to know if there were
any Indians there, and he needed somebody to find out about it.
In the second place, superior officers often consider it best not
to explain reasons for orders given. This disinclination to give
reasons for his orders was said to have been customary with
Custer. In this respect, Sergeant Ferdinand Culbertson's testimony at the Reno court-martial trial, which included the following, may be applied to the Benteen case:

> I heard Captain Weir ask Captain Moylan if, when he was
> adjutant, General Custer gave him any particular orders
> about anything. Captain Moylan said, "No," that when he
> was adjutant General Custer never told him what he was
> going to do, that he would order him to tell the company
> commanders to go such-and-such a place, and that was all.

The two possibilities as to the location of Indians developed
into three possibilities as Custer and his main column marched
on down through the vacated campsite at the forks of Reno
Creek. The continuation of the Indian trail below that site veered
to the southward as it led on toward the Little Bighorn River
nearby. But the camp that had been located by sight—having
been seen from high points as the soldiers were marching down
Reno Creek—was about four miles north from where this tributary
flows into the Little Bighorn. Were there camps both above and
below the mouth of Reno Creek, and several miles apart?

Once more a reference to the chapter telling of the Indian
movements is appropriate. On June 18 the Indians left the forks
of Reno Creek. Planning to go southward up the Little Bighorn,
they set up their next camp on its banks two or three miles above
the mouth of Reno Creek. But, instead of going up the valley,

they changed their plans and moved down it for four or five miles. This move was made on the 24th, and the next morning, the 25th, the soldiers came. The Indian trail made by the move of the 24th was on the west side of the Little Bighorn, and therefore it could not be seen by the soldiers marching down Reno Creek, which flows into the east side. The only trail then in view of the soldiers was the one leading to the region above the mouth of Reno Creek.

So, Custer made another division of his forces. He sent Major Reno and Troops A, M, and G, with the Indian scouts to accompany them, on down the south side of Reno Creek. They were to cross to the west side of the Little Bighorn and attack whatever Indians they might encounter. Custer himself, with Troops E, C, L, I, and F, left Reno Creek and turned to go northwestward over the hills, in the direction of the tipis that had been seen.

But what tipis had been seen?

Yet another reference to the Indian movements will be helpful. As we know, six separate tribal camp circles were arranged in a long group on the west side of the Little Bighorn River, the southernmost circle being that of the Hunkpapa Sioux, and the northernmost that of the Northern Cheyenne. The four intermediate circles were all Sioux.

Cottonwood trees in full leaf along the river and high bluffs and hills along its east bank hid all of the five Sioux camps from the view of whoever might be east of the bluffs immediately bordering the river. There is no high point on the divide to the east, nor anywhere else in that direction, from which any of the five Sioux campsites could have been seen. Conversely, one who stands on any of those sites and looks toward the distant eastern hills cannot see any of them, not even the highest points. He can see only the bluffs just across the river in front of him. Those who disbelieve this should go and see for themselves.

But the Northern Cheyenne camp was in plain view from the hills for several miles to the east of the river and might have been seen from high points still further away. There were neither trees nor bluffs east of it. On the contrary, just across the river east of it was a broad coulee and a long slope toward the hill country further eastward. The Northern Cheyenne camp was thus the Indian camp Custer and his scouts had seen, and this was the camp—and doubtless the only camp—he had in mind when he parted from Reno and started across the hills toward it.

It may be that Custer was expecting Reno to strike this same

camp, the only one that could be seen. He then had no way of
knowing that Reno was going to be met by a host of Hunkpapa
two or three miles up the river from the camp he had seen. If
it really was his intention to strike this visible camp from below
while Reno would strike it from above, then the bitter accusation
that he thrust Reno into a hopeless charge while Custer and his
men dallied in the hills is utterly confuted. From the point of
separation, with Reno going the valley route, the two detachments
would have arrived at the Cheyenne camp at about the same
time.

Custer's first view of the great combined encampment came
after he and Reno were both well advanced on their separate
courses to the attack. Then it was that some of the Reno men saw
him on the bluffs just east of the river. Then it was that he sent
the hurry-up message to Benteen. Then it was that, instead of the
1,500 Indians estimated in his conversations with his officers, he
found himself plunging into about 12,000 of them.

The Reno men tell of Custer's waving his big white hat at them.
All of the interpretations of that gesture have been that he was
cheering them in their charge. It may be, though, that his amaze-
ment at the discovery of so many Indians caused him to try to
convey to Reno some reversal order. It is not altogether improbable that the supposed encouraging wave of the hat was really a
vehement prohibitory gesticulation, and that it was accompanied
by a shouted admonition, such as: "Stop! Wait until Benteen
comes!"

On any summer day, at the site of the Custer battlefield, one
may hear from casual visitors many belittlings of Custer for what
they term his military mismanagement. A frequently heard comment is: "He ought to have kept his forces together for the
attack."

Good idea, casual visitor. But, go on and tell us more. Where
should the attack have been made? Should Custer have led all
of his forces up the South Reno Creek trail? Or should he have
stuck to the main Indian trail as it turned southward from the
mouth of the main Reno Creek? Or should he have massed his
men and attacked the only camp actually seen, which was four
miles north of the mouth of Reno Creek, and which later proved
to be only the Cheyenne camp circle? In other words: Where
were the Indians? How many of them were in the region? Were
they all in one camp, or in camps at various places? Imagine
yourself in Custer's place, with his lack of knowledge of the true
case—and decide at once, as he had to do. Also, keep in mind

that, if the full regiment goes en masse to the wrong place, its commander renders himself ridiculous.

We now know how many Indians were involved, and we also know precisely where they were and how their camps were arranged. But it was not practicable for Custer to know. It is not fair, then, to belittle his decisions, made on the scant basis of fact he had to use, while we draw our wise conclusions on the foolproof basis afforded by the knowledge we now have available to us.

There has been much debate as to precisely where the Custer detachment moved in the last mile or so to the place of its final stand at the battle ridge. There has been much theorizing about the possibility that it went down a narrow coulee now known as the south prong of Medicine Tail Coulee, just east of and almost parallel to the bluffs along the river. This theory supposes that when they arrived close to the river, where the coulee opens out just across the river from the Cheyenne campsite, they were met by the Indians. It is supposed that the fighting began there, and that Custer gradually retreated to the ridge.

But the Indians are unanimous in their statements that the Custer soldiers were first seen moving at a trot on a high and long ridge running almost parallel with the river and almost two miles east of the Cheyenne camp. The Cheyenne watched them, and the soldiers had the Cheyenne in full view. A few warriors went out in that direction and exchanged long-distance shots with the soldiers. Other warriors—Cheyenne and Sioux—followed. More of them, and yet more of them, lashed their ponies through the waters of the river and went tearing on to meet the white invaders. It was not until after the soldiers had gone a considerable distance beyond that part of the ridge nearest the Cheyenne camp that the column swerved leftward to a lower ridge nearer the river. By this time there was a vast throng of warriors at their front, while others were beginning to encircle them. They took up their position on this ridge, and there a pitched battle began. There it also ended. The soldiers never got any nearer to the river than they were when they died.

The southern prong of Medicine Tail Coulee afforded much the shorter and easier route of approach for Custer. Its upper beginning is near the bluff where the Reno men saw him as he waved his hat. It was in this vicinity that Trumpeter Martin left to carry the hurry-up message to Benteen. This last man to leave the Custer detachment is quoted as having said that they were just then about to start down the coulee. It is quite natural to believe that such was the case. This allows room for speculation as to how it came about that the first view the Indians had of Custer's men was far out on the ridge.

One explanation might be as follows. The troops were actually about to start down the coulee, but when Custer saw the great size of the camp he decided that the approach he contemplated would surely be repulsed. He waved a warning to Reno, either to change his charge into a retreat or to make a careful stand. Then he took his own detachment to the high ridge, in full view of the Indians, as a threatening demonstration that would draw them to him or scare them into flight, thus relieving the strain on Reno. Then, having gone along the ridge, he found no place where his column could descend from it until the men arrived at the lower ridge where they actually did descend and begin to fight.

Another explanation, however, and seemingly the best one, is this. The decision not to go down the coulee was based upon thoughts of the great number of untrained men who would thus be brought into a sudden encounter with a force just discovered to be vastly superior in numbers. Perhaps Custer had seen indications of unsteadiness among the Reno men as they went into that initial combat that resulted in their swift and calamitous defeat. It was his special business, at the critical moment of his own contemplated approach, to note the mental state of his own men. Doubtless he did so, and it is highly probable that he saw among them many signs of unsteadiness, trepidation, or distinct perturbation—premonitions of the uncontrollable panic that afterwards did develop among them. He therefore decided that he definitely would not lead men in that state of mind into a sudden frontal attack on that immense camp. Instead, he would take them along the hills to make a gradual approach that might enable them to achieve some degree of composure. Coupling this thought with the idea of enticing the Indians out to meet him, and thus to relieve the pressure on the Reno men, it seems likely that when all of the Indians did come out to meet him he felt that his tactics in this respect had been a thorough success.

Both General Sheridan, the division commander, and General Sherman, the supreme commander of the armies of the United States, reviewed Custer's entire conduct at the Little Bighorn and exonerated him from all blame. It appears that the most active and severe critic was Major Brisbin. Among his utterances was a long letter to Godfrey, in 1892, which was made public. The letter refers to Custer in such terms as "this wild man" and "the insufferable ass."

Major Brisbin's letter says that he was present during the officer conferences—between Terry, Gibbon, Custer, and others—on the steamboat *Far West* at the mouth of the Rosebud. He tells of a map being drawn to show Custer where he was to go up the Rosebud. He says that Terry, being near-sighted, requested him, Brisbin, to blue-pencil the line where Custer was to proceed to the southward and to stick pins along the line, and he did so. The letter claims that Brisbin urged Custer to take the artillery pieces, and it claims that Brisbin also originated the idea that his four cavalry troops be sent with Custer, and that Terry go along as the supreme commander. Brisbin writes of his own march, under Gibbon's general leadership, up the Yellowstone and on to the Little Bighorn. In his reference to the time when Gibbon was sick on the steamboat and had left Brisbin in temporary general command, the substitute leader boasts of his having speeded up the rate of travel. He writes: "I rushed the Montana column," and, further on in his letter, "I pushed and pushed." This is not consistent with his beratings of Custer for hurrying.

Although the Brisbin strictures deserve consideration, they do not deserve full credit. Evidently, he also was longing for a battle that might bring him military honors. Maybe his sticking of pins along the blue-pencil line steering Custer to the extreme upper Rosebud and beyond was a Brisbin idea for tightening Terry's written suggestion into the semblance of a positive command. The Brisbin proposal that he and his Second Cavalry troops accompany Custer may have been regarded by Custer as altogether in Brisbin's self-interest. The "generous offer" to let Custer have the artillery may have been construed by him, reasonably, as designed to hinder his progress, as it actually did hinder Brisbin's progress over the hills east of the Bighorn.

Many veteran soldier survivors of that Little Bighorn affair carried on bitter disputes concerning it throughout their subsequent lives. It is notable that on each point in controversy the usual alignment of the disputants has been in accordance with their several personal interests. Therefore, although their testimony as to facts is of the highest importance, their conclusions may be regarded as subject to prejudice. Consider some of these controversial alignments:

The Gibbon-Brisbin soldiers have been practically unanimous in condemning Custer for his departure from the Rosebud course, as blue-penciled and pin-stuck by Major Brisbin. They have maintained that therein Custer flagrantly disobeyed Terry's orders. On the other hand, the surviving men of the Seventh Cavalry have been practically unanimous in approving the turn he made in his course. They have maintained firmly that in his action he did not disobey any positive order, that he was authorized to use his full discretion in the matter, and, further, that it was his paramount duty to follow the Indian trail, to find them, and to fight them.

The Reno men in the valley fight have been in general accord in commending their leader for the hurried flight from that scene. On the other hand, many of the Benteen soldiers who were scouting southward at that time have expressed opinions that the failure of the Reno men to hold their ground in the valley was the one great delinquency which caused the general disaster.

The combined Reno-Benteen men on the hilltop have been close to unanimity in their expressions of belief that it was impossible for them to have gone to join Custer, even if they had known of his location and his distress. Since all of the Custer men died, their opinions on that point have never been voiced to us. It is probable, however, that if a few of them had escaped the general slaughter, they would have contended ever thereafter that the combined Reno-Benteen forces could have gone to Custer's aid, and ought to have done so.

Before the encounter with the Indians, no thoughts were voiced by the soldiers of the possibility of a serious reverse. The whole talk had been of schemes to catch the hostiles and to compel a fight, as catching up with them and drawing them into combat had been the main problems in preceding campaigns against the Indians. All outward indications among the Seventh Cavalry were of unqualified confidence. Up to the time of the discovery of the trail on the Rosebud Valley, the officers had been guessing that only a few Indians were off the reservations, that they might find none at all, and that the regiment would be back at the home post in August.

It appears plain that Custer himself had no thought of any possibility of a devastating blow being delivered to his regiment in the campaign. His letters to his wife, as the expedition progressed, exude his usual buoyancy of spirit. In an early letter he wrote: "I have about made up my mind that when I go on expeditions like this you are to go too." At the post he and his wife had planned for her to come on a steamboat carrying military supplies to the mouth of the Powder River. But Captain Marsh, commander of the boat, refused to take her. Custer wrote to her of his disappointment. Her book *Boots and Saddles* contains that letter and others from him. On June 17, at the mouth of the Tongue River, and eight days before the battle, his long letter told her of the delights of travel in the Yellowstone country. He glowed: "You might just as well be here as not."

Genuine confidence is demonstrated in all of his last known actions. They provide good reason for dissenting with the accusation that, smothering all interests except his own, he ruthlessly took his men into a conflict he knew to be desperately dangerous. The accusation is also strongly refuted by the fact that with him were four of his relatives: Captain Tom Custer, a junior brother; Lieutenant Calhoun, a brother-in-law; Boston Custer, his 19-year-old youngest brother; and Autie Reed, a 16-year-old nephew. Boston was the foragemaster during the wagon train march from Dakota. Autie was a herder for the beef cattle on that journey. They were civilian employees, not soldiers, and neither of them was on duty for the march up the Rosebud in immediate pursuit of the Indians. It would have been quite natural to leave them at the base camp on the Yellowstone. But they continued on with the regiment, for they were expecting a grand frolic—maybe to get a scalp or a warbonnet to show to the folks back at home.

When the culminating dash towards the Indians' camps began, it would have been quite natural for Custer, if he sensed special danger, to compel these two young civilian kinfolks to stay behind with the pack train, in comparative security. But, no. He fully expected to win, and he would allow them to share in the fun of watching the comic antics of the Indians wildly scrambling to escape the soldiers' bullets. He would let these two boys see the whole amusing show.

And they saw it. Two days afterward their naked, mutilated, and putrefying bodies were found with other gory human remnants scattered over the sagebrush hills and gulches. And now, among the marble slabs for the soldiers on that battlefield, are marble slabs for Boston Custer and Autie Reed.

THE CHARGES AGAINST RENO

Major Marcus A. Reno, the only major in the Seventh Cavalry at the Little Bighorn, has been condemned by many reviewers as the one sole individual cause of the military catastrophe there. Two special counts have been enumerated in the charges against him. It has been contended that he ought not to have halted in his first charge toward the Hunkpapa camp or, having halted, he should have kept his stand and held the Indians off instead of retreating a mile or so to the hilltop across the river at the eastward. In addition, since he did go to the hilltop, it has been contended that he ought to have gone on northward and joined Custer. It has been claimed that his feeling of personal malice toward Custer was a factor in his decision not to go. But the principal criticism against him has been that his military management showed gross incompetence, that he was the one weak link in a regimental chain which otherwise was strong. Some charges of cowardice were added to the general charges of incompetence.

It appears that the association between Custer and Reno in previous times had not been cordial. It appears also that many officers in the Seventh Cavalry regarded both Custer and Reno with feelings not altogether cordial. Custer's brusque and derisive ways generated unpleasant reactions to him. Reno's habits and general conduct brought upon him feelings of disrespect or of active dislike. Probably, though, there were then, and no doubt are now, many army regiments whose officers have personal antipathies towards each other. But, regularly—and quite naturally—all personal antipathies are smothered or are utterly forgotten when the time comes for alignment against a common foe. There has been no open allegation that either Major Reno or any other officer ever failed to do his full duty under Custer in any of the previous military operations of the Seventh Cavalry in any combat engagement. Probably, there never was any such default. At all events, it needed neither reprehensible weakness nor contemptible cowardice to cause Reno to stop his first charge toward the Indian camps and, a little later, to hasten to the hilltop refuge. It needed neither weakness, cowardice, nor malice to cause him to say on that hilltop. Whether his course in both instances was as a result of his virtues or his faults, in each instance his course was the best one.

Custer ordered Reno to cross the Little Bighorn and to charge down the valley upon the Indians. The crossing was about three miles southeast and up the river from the nearest camp circle, that of the Hunkpapa. The Reno detachment consisted of Troops M, A, and G, numbering about 112 men. The officers of these three troops were Captains Moylan and French, and Lieutenants De Rudio, Wallace, and McIntosh. Lieutenant Hodgson was with them as Reno's adjutant. About 20 Arikara Indian scouts and 4 Crow Indian scouts, under the command of Lieutenants Varnum and Hare, were ordered by Custer to accompany Reno. Other scouts accompanying him were Charles Reynolds, Fred Girard, George Herendeen, and Bob Jackson, who was half white and half Piegan Blackfeet Indian. The regiment's Sioux interpreter, a black named Isaiah Dorman, also accompanied him. Dr. Porter, the regiment's assistant surgeon, and Dr. DeWolf, a contract surgeon, were with this detachment as its medical officers. So the total number of men who started with Reno—including himself and counting officers, enlisted men, Indian and other scouts, interpreter, and doctors—was about 152.

All of them were on horseback. After they had crossed to the west side of the river, they started at a trot or a gallop toward the Indian camps. They had gone but a short distance when a few Indians on their ponies skirted across their front, while others appeared at the ravines on their left. As the soldiers proceeded further, other Indians, and yet others, appeared in view as obstacles. About that time the Arikara and Crow Indian scouts broke ranks and scattered. Some of them—perhaps the brightest ones among them—turned back to escape. Other scouts remained to fight, but to fight in their own way, as individuals darting here or there to make coups or to capture Sioux ponies from the herds in the valley. Varnum and Hare found themselves without any followers, so they joined the soldiers.

The number of warriors coming out from the Hunkpapa camp increased rapidly as the soldiers proceeded onward. The warriors sent some bullets, at long range, without harmful effect. But as the soldiers advanced, the number of opposing warriors continued to increase rapidly, and the bullets they sent increased in number and sang closer. While the warriors were then staying mainly on the defensive, additions to their array were flowing out constantly and in big bands. The great extent of the camps, much greater than had been expected, just then came into the view of Reno and his men. Thoughts of making an aggressive charge into that multitude with his small forces were transformed into thoughts of preserving his men, if possible, from speedy extinction. About a quarter of a mile from the south edge of the Hunkpapa camp circle, Reno ordered a halt.

All were ordered to dismount. Men were detailed to take charge of the horses, one man for each four horses, about 29 or 30 men for all of them. The mounts were led to a clump of brush and larger timber to the right, and at the border of a deep slough or long loop of the river projecting westward from the main stream. The remaining men and their officers formed a skirmish line, the men about five yards apart, with the line running out in a southwesterly direction toward the hills. All the men dropped down to lie prone upon the ground, and all of them lay facing the main body of warriors. Among the men there was a general murmur of satisfaction at having been stopped from a charge in which the whole detachment might have been swallowed up in a few minutes. Some of the officers spoke out at once to praise Reno for having ordered the halt. Not only then but ever afterward, all of the survivors who were there have been in agreement that a successful continuation of that charge was entirely impracticable.

Up to that time, no bullet or arrow had harmed any soldier. Some of the men claimed they had seen Custer and one or two companions on the bluffs just across the river to the eastward. It was therefore expected that his detachment would be going into action immediately, and that the attention of these warriors would be drawn toward him or would be divided. Gradually, however, the warriors worked around the skirmish line and toward its rear. Also, they gradually approached closer. A soldier was hit, then another, and another. After a time—generally estimated at from 15 to 20 minutes—the skirmish line was pivoted backward at its left, then the men were ordered to retreat to the horses in the timber.

Although there were indications of a loss of soldierly coolness on the skirmish line and during the retreat to the horses, there was no marked break in carrying out the maneuvers. It may be that this preservation of order was as a result of the warriors not pressing them too hard at that time. There was also the expectation that Custer was about to make his attack, or the probability that he had already begun it. Thus far the Indians had held themselves in check, but their numbers were constantly augmenting and they were shifting steadily into an encirclement. As the soldiers reached the timber position, a mass of Indian horsemen swung around at the south and toward the east, while to the west side, where the skirmish line had been, there was a move forward to occupy the vacated ground. Plainly, Reno and his men were being surrounded. Moreover, the number of Indians in the surrounding circle, with more of them coming in an unceasing flow, was a situation rendering mental agitation excusable.

When Custer sent his adjutant, Lieutenant William Cooke, to order Reno to cross the river and ride to the charge, the order was accompanied by a supplementary commitment: "and the whole outfit will support you." Practically all of the military men offering opinions on this point have maintained that Custer's evident design to make a simultaneous charge at the opposite end of the camps was an attempt to give the promised support. But Reno and his officers expected that the Custer detachment would follow not far behind, or that it would be somewhere else very near at hand when the charge was made. While the men were on the skirmish line, or at about that time, Reno learned that Custer was in the hills on the east side of the river. While Reno and his men were in the timber, with the Indians surrounding them there, he still expected that Custer would suddenly spring a big surprise and that all would end happily for the white men.

While the Indians were still not crowding close to the soldiers in the timber shelter, the warriors' shooting appeared to be increasing in effectiveness. Bloody Knife, an Arikara scout, was killed as he stood beside Major Reno, blood and brains from the victim bespattering the officer's clothing. Charley Reynolds, a white scout, was picked off and fell dead just outside the border of the trees. One or two enlisted men were wounded. Dr. Porter found something to do in his line of work. Emotion among the men was increasing. It must be considered that this was the first battle against Indians ever experienced by a very large percentage of them, and that a considerable percentage of them were inexperienced in every way as soldiers. More than half of the officers had never before been in an Indian battle, and these must have exhibited some degree of agitation that was noticed by their men. Major Reno manifested doubt and indecision. But he had good grounds for having such feelings. Why didn't Custer come?

Much of the condemnation of Reno's vacating the timber position has been based—as such condemnations are often based—upon knowledge gained afterward. It was later learned that as soon as Reno and his men got to the hilltop, every one of the Indians quit him and went to fight Custer. It was learned—in a retrospective review of the events—that the Benteen detachment and the pack train arrived on the hill and joined Reno soon after the Indians fighting him in the timber and during his retreat had gone. Evaluating these events after they had occurred, it became evident that if Reno had held his timber position, with the Indians remaining around him, Custer would have gone on to attack the lower end of the camps, with little or no opposition there, instead of being met out on the hills—as he was met—by a great force of opposing warriors. Further, the Benteen detachment would have appeared at that time in view on the hills just across the river, a mile or so from Reno. The pressure on Reno then would have been greatly relaxed, or would have been broken up entirely, and a general advantage to the soldiers would probably have ensued.

But all that Reno in the timber on the west side of the river knew about the Custer detachment was that they were somewhere on the east side of the river. He did not know exactly where they were or exactly what Custer expected to do—in fact, it appears that Custer was compelled to make a variation upon his original plan. Reno had no knowledge of where Benteen was, or where Benteen was going, or what Benteen was expected to do —and, in fact, Benteen himself did not know just what was expected of him and his detachment. Reno did not know what would be the course of the lagging pack train, bearing the ammunition stores. Surrounded by the Indians, he could not send out any courier to obtain information. Considering that none of that important information was available to Major Reno in the timber, how long should he have stayed there and kept on in the fight against the Indians? How many hours? How many minutes?

Some extracts from testimony at the Reno court-martial trial may help in understanding Reno's plight in the timber. Lieutenant George Wallace's testimony included the following: "I think Reno did the only thing possible under the circumstances. If we had remained in the timber, all would have been killed." Lieutenant Charles Varnum testified: "The position in the timber was as good as any on the left bank, but I don't think he had men enough to hold it." Captain Myles Moylan's testimony on this point was: "In my judgment, the command, without assistance, would have been annihilated in the timber." Sergeant Ferdinand Culbertson said: "I don't think Major Reno could have held the timber but a few minutes." Lieutenant Luther Hare expressed himself thus: "Major Reno stayed in the timber till all hope of support from Custer vanished." All of these witnesses were with Reno in the timber.

All of the publicly expressed opinions as to Reno's holding his timber position—either for or against his course—have omitted consideration of the kind of soldiers he had with him. This omission has also occurred in reviewing all other aspects of the battle of the Little Bighorn. Any man who has served in any army during combat times knows that untrained and inexperienced soldiers are not merely of little use, but that they are a positive hindrance to the trained and experienced men. The veterans have not only to fight the enemy, but they are also burdened with weak comrades leaning upon them for support or breaking combat rules that must then be enforced upon them by the veterans. It does not need many such undisciplined delinquents to wreck the effectiveness of any army unit if it comes under severe strain. The Reno detachment was subjected to such a severe strain, and there were in their ranks more than enough greenhorns to wreck its effectiveness. And they began to act in a way that showed they were surely going to do so. Reno was therefore faced with a choice. Should he stay and allow an evidently impending panic to develop into a general collapse before his eyes? Or should he try to do something in an effort to salvage what he could? It would have been reasonable for him to decide that the result of a bold dash to get out of the Indian encirclement would not be any more disastrous, and might be much less disastrous, than remaining in the timber. That was the decision he did make.

An excess of men, rather than not enough of them, was the main trouble in the timber, as was the case with Custer when the Indians surrounded him. If, instead of the 9 officers and 112 enlisted men in the Reno detachment, there had been about 5 officers and 60 men—the right kind of officers and men—they probably could have held their ground and would have done so.

As will be seen in a subsequent chapter, on many another occasion, at other places, a few cool and determined white men fought successfully for hours, even throughout the day, against numbers of Indian warriors proportionally greater in numbers than those that Reno and his men faced. But Reno, as well as all of his officers and his veteran enlisted men, could see that the general feeling in their detachment just then was far from one of coolness and determination. It was clear that that body of emotional men could not hold its ground.

The length of time that they stayed in the timber has been estimated by survivors at from 20 to 30 minutes. The number of Indians around them was estimated by Reno at 600 to 700. Lieutenant Hare's estimate was 1,000. Sergeant Culbertson put the number at 1,000 to 1,200. It appears that Major Reno vacillated in determining whether to stay or to go. It may be that his vacillation was caused by reversals in the behavior of his men. They may have alternated between hopefulness and despair. He may have felt that his final decision depended upon their mental condition becoming settled one way or the other. Practically all subsequent reviews of the event clearly indicate that the despair became predominant.

A general confusion then prevailed. Reno conferred with some of his officers. The conference, however, did not take the form of a gathering, but was conducted by shouting to and fro, while each troop officer remained with his own men. Word went around that Reno had ordered that the horses be mounted. But either the word did not get all the way around, or else in some quarters there was an understanding that the order had been countermanded. Concerted action, therefore, did not take place until Reno himself and the troop nearest him began to mount their horses and form a column. Then all the others rushed to mount in preparation for moving out. The rush was so great that some of the horses were frightened, broke loose, and ran away. A few of the men were thus left on foot.

In some approximation of orderly column array, the horses were at once whipped into a gallop. The course taken was almost due east, toward the bluffs where some of Reno's men had seen Custer at the time they were about to charge toward the camps. This next horseback dash, although escape was the prime object, was in the nature of a charge, for in order to reach their objective—the hill—they had to break through the Indian ranks on that side. At first it seemed encouraging when the Indians shrank back or turned aside. But, as the soldiers rode on to pass them, all these warriors, as well as other warriors who had been following the white men, crowded beside them, behind them, and among them.

The soldiers' horses were rather tired, as veterans who were there have attested. The horses had been marching daily over rough country throughout the five preceding weeks. They had traveled over a considerable extent of such rough country during the preceding three days. On that particular day they had already traveled far enough to render any horse leg weary. The last part of that travel had been a gallop of almost three miles toward the Indian camps.

The soldiers themselves must have been tired. They had made a march during the preceding night. After only two or three hours of sleep—probably, for many, no more than a disturbed and restless reclining—the march had been resumed and had continued for four or five hours, up to the moment of the dismounting to form the skirmish line. After such a draining of the vital batteries of energy, no man could be anywhere near either his physical or his mental best. Doubtless, this was an important factor in the breakdown of composure that occurred during the timber fighting, and it was still operative when they were trying to get away from the timber.

On the Indian side, both the warriors and their ponies were in fresh condition. Up to the moment of the alarm being given that soldiers were approaching their camps, they had been engaged in the regular routine of their daily life for long enough to have their vital batteries stored to full capacity. Practically all of them must have been at their best in capability. Even had the warriors been naturally inferior as individual fighters, their advantage in being fully rested might have enabled them to outwit and outdo their fatigued enemies.

Thus, the warriors on their swift ponies found it easy to catch up with the fleeing soldiers, and the soldiers for their part found it impossible to evade them. The pursuers jeered the pursued, and they used the lashes or handles of their pony whips for striking coup blows upon them. Indian bullets or arrows rained into the column. Soldiers, or horses, or both, went down. One such victim was Lieutenant Donald McIntosh, who fell soon after the column started. Others fell as it proceeded. There was little shooting by the soldiers during the rush to the river. Their energies were primarily devoted to escaping. Most of the damage was done to them just as they reached the river, while they were crossing it, and as they were scrambling up the bluffs on its east side.

They had followed a buffalo trail to a buffalo ford. The same trail and ford are still used today by domestic cattle and horses. At the ford there were jump-off banks all along the stream both above and below the single-file buffalo trail which led gradually down to the water's edge. The banks were from three to five feet above the water, and the water there was between three and four feet deep. So at any point the vertical distance from the top of the bank to the bottom of the water was between six and nine feet. The river was about 75 feet across.

There was a jam, of course, immediately after the leading horses arrived at the ford. There was room for only one horse at a time to follow the single-file buffalo trench sloping into the water. The column broke into complete disorder. Every individual soldier began to think solely of his own welfare. Looking after his own welfare in these circumstances consisted in trying to find a place where he could get into and across the river. Men sprang from their horses, dropped their rifles, and jumped into the water —if they were not killed before the jump could be made. Others, remaining on their horses, urged the animals to jump. Some were crowded off the edge by other horses plunging against them.

In this frenzied jumble, the white men became easy victims for the red men. Soldiers were shot, stabbed, and clubbed to death without making any, or but little, show of resistance. Some were stunned or more seriously disabled by the jumping or tumbling of their horses off the steep banks. These also were shot, stabbed, or clubbed to death. All who got across the stream were followed. Lieutenant Hodgson was wounded while he was crossing, and killed just after he reached the other shore. Dr. DeWolf was killed as he was climbing the hill on the other side. A few others fell after they had crossed the water.

The angle of the slope from the river up to the hilltop varies from about 30 to 60 degrees, according to whether the climb is made along one of the gullies or along one of the gradually sloping ridges. Up these gullies and ridges the soldiers clambered, some of them leading their horses, others letting loose their mounts, not wanting to be delayed by them. The Indians sent bullets across the river and towards the men going up the hill. A few of the men were hit, but the distance and the better position of the soldiers for returning the fire prevented too much harm from being done by these shots. In 1929 the author, in good physical condition, made a test by going on foot from the east bank of the river to the top of the hill. Taking a sloping ridge course, and hurrying all the way, the hilltop was reached in exactly ten minutes.

As the soldiers arrived on the hill, they were placed at stations at which they could make a stand. Many warriors had already crossed above and below the ford and were on adjacent hills. Other warriors were coming across the river. The firing toward the soldiers was resumed, or it was continued. After a time estimated at from 10 to 30 minutes, the Benteen detachment arrived. His men were deployed to take up the burden of the fighting while the Reno men were being redeployed. A few minutes afterward, the Indians began to leave the scene. They turned their ponies to go back across the river or else to go northward along the hills on the east side of the river. It was not long before all of them had disappeared.

Officers of the Reno and Benteen detachments—all then under the command of Reno—began to express their feelings to each other about the situation. One expression was: "Why are we staying here?" Another was: "What's the matter with Custer that he doesn't send word to tell us what to do?" Captain Weir and Lieutenant Edgerly, who had been with Benteen, took their troop and started northward. They sent back word that they could hear firing going on in that direction. There were some whisperings that if Reno did not take his entire command down in that direction, or take some other positive and aggressive action, Custer would "get after him with a sharp stick."

The pack train arrived on the hill. This arrival took place between an hour and two hours after the Benteen detachment had come. About the time that the pack train came, some men who had been left behind in the flight from the valley rejoined their comrades on the hill. The delayed ones were Herendeen, a scout, and 11 enlisted men. All of them were on foot, and three of them were wounded. There were now 10 or 11 wounded men among the Reno forces on the hill.

A thorough check of the lists of the Reno detachment was made. It disclosed an absence of 4 officers and 30 enlisted men. The officers were Lieutenants Hodgson, McIntosh, DeRudio, and Dr. DeWolf. In addition to the missing soldiers, other absentees were three scouts, Reynolds, Jackson, and Girard, and the interpreter, Isaiah Dorman. Two Crow and several Arikara were present. All the other Indian scouts had fled, except for three Arikara who had been killed.

Thus, the original Reno detachment was found to be considerably decimated. There had been 9 officers, besides the 2 doctors, and 112 enlisted men. The hilltop roll call showed the presence of 6 officers, 1 doctor, and 82 enlisted men, about 71 or 72 of these enlisted men being uninjured. The original man-count of 152—officers, enlisted men, and all others—was found to be reduced to about 100. Deducting the wounded, the number able to fight was 90.

Benteen had about 125 officers and enlisted men, with no other additional men in his detachment. Captain Thomas McDougall had about 120 enlisted men in his rearguard, or pack train guard. Lieutenant Edward Mathey had about 70 soldiers and 4 or 5 civilians for handling the 160 pack mules and the baggage borne by them. When all of these men came under Reno's command, he had a total of about 410 men of all kinds who each had guns and ammunition and could use them. That number excluded the ten wounded men, who were a hindrance rather than a help.

After suggestions and then urgings by various officers—with the urgings being carried almost to the point of contumacious insubordination—Major Reno finally gave passive consent to a movement of his combined forces in the direction in which Custer was believed to have gone, and from where the firing had been heard. His passive or reluctant consent was manifested simply by his joining in a movement that he had not positively ordered, but which had already started. Nobody indicated any thought that the purpose of going was to relieve Custer from impending disaster. It could just as well have been to seek help for themselves—and probably this was the idea in the minds of some. But the main idea undoubtedly was to renew the fighting against the Indians, under whatever conditions they might be encountered, as well as to get into touch with Custer so that he might give them further orders.

It seems, though, that there was good reason for Reno's feeling that he ought to stay for a longer time on the hilltop, in plain view of the valley where they had been fighting. Herendeen and 11 enlisted men had come to him there about two hours after they had been left behind in the valley. How many more of the absentees would come straggling in to him if he should stay there in view for another two hours? Of the missing officers, he knew that Hodgson and DeWolf had been killed. Of the missing enlisted men, nobody knew how many of them might yet be alive, wounded or unwounded, watching their comrades safe on the hilltop and trying to get to them. Lieutenant McIntosh had been seen to fall, but was he dead? Nobody knew for a certainty. Was Lieutenant DeRudio dead or alive, wounded or unharmed? Nobody knew. Were all of the missing civilians accounted for to a certainty? They were not.

It was known that some of the men left in the valley were wounded but not dead at the time of their abandonment. Major Reno's trial testimony included this statement: "I do not know what was done to the wounded that were left on the plain. The Indians would not permit us to take care of them. I could make no effort to take them out, and none was made." Private Slaper's story, which appears in one of E. A. Brininstool's published interviews, tells of an illustrative incident. His special comrade, a man named Klotzbucher, was wounded during the fighting in the timber. When the detachment was leaving there, the wounded man was given a canteen of water and left to take care of himself as best he might. Dr. Porter's testimony at the Reno trial relates that he was attending a wounded man when the order came to mount the horses to leave the timber. The doctor quit his patient and joined the rush. His testimony adds: "No wounded men were brought in from the bottom. Seven or eight hung to their horses, but dropped off when they got to the top of the hill."

The leaving of wounded men when retiring from a field of battle against Indians was quite a different matter from leaving them to the mercies of men of their own race. Custer had been much criticized for leaving the Washita battlefield without knowing what had become of Major Elliott and his detachment. There has been talk that General Terry, at the Rosebud conference with Custer, urged him: "Do not abandon any wounded men." That admonition, unqualified by any reservation, seems too rigid. It was not like Terry, if indeed he said anything on the subject, to be so tersely dogmatic. But the declarations that he did say something indicate that the abandonment of wounded men to the "mercy" of Indians was regarded by all soldiers with a feeling of horror. Reno already had left some men known to be wounded and not dead. He must have felt that it would be utterly heartless to go on further away from them.

In connection with the condemnation of Reno for his failure to go to Custer's relief, there have been pathetic references to Custer's having had his men fire volleys in a way that was well known to all as a call for help. It is entirely probable that such volleys were fired. But it is not probable that they could be heard and understood by the men with Reno on the hill. As the crow flies, the distance between the Custer monument and the Reno Hill monument is four and a quarter miles. Neither point or its immediate surroundings can be seen from the other point or its surroundings. If all of them had been quiet and listening, the men on Reno Hill might have heard and understood such volleys. But there never has been any statement that all of them, nor any considerable number of them, established such listening period. On the contrary, there was probably a continual din of talk, much of it excited, and most of it concerning what had occurred in the valley.

Even if, however, there had been a concerted plan to keep quiet and listen, there was no knowing beforehand at precisely what time such a period of silence would be needed. Even if some one man or some few men had caught vague sounds of volleying, a general notification of this fact and the establishment of an ensuing period of silence might have taken up enough time for the volleying to cease, so that the listening would have been unrewarded. Or even if, by an unforeseen coincidence, all the men had been perfectly quiet and listening at just the right time, there was no way for them to suppress the interference caused by the constant minglings of many kinds of noises coming from the 160 pack mules and more than 400 horses in their midst.

Various men who were on Reno Hill declared afterward that they had heard volleys of distress coming from the Custer forces. General Godfrey, writing in 1921 for the Montana Historical Society collections, discusses the matter. He says that somebody hearing them remarked: "Custer is giving it to them for all he is worth." This indicates that whatever shooting was heard just then was regarded simply as the sound of a lively engagement, and as a sign that Custer was doing well. The Godfrey writing adds: "I have little doubt now that these volleys were fired by Custer's orders as signals of distress and to show where he was." It should be noted that, in Godfrey's phrase "I have little doubt now," the word "now" has reference to 1921, the time of his writing, 45 years after the battle. It is fair to presume that all of the others who may have heard shooting from the Custer forces also did not think of it at the time as a distress signal until subsequent discoveries prompted the idea.

Despite Reno's reluctance, a general movement began to move toward where Custer was supposed to be. But the wounded men hindered their progress. Because of them, it took longer to get ready to start. After the start was made, the march had to be a slow one, and the demeanor of the force did not in the least suggest aggressive intent. Captain Moylan's troop, in particular, could not travel at the pace set by the leaders. The wounded men had to be carried by comrades on foot. Moylan testified that it took four to carry one, while Lieutenant Wallace said it took six to carry one.

In many other instances of a similar character, military movements were halted because of the wounded men. An instance occurred only eight days before the Reno crisis, during the Crook battle on the Rosebud. At a certain stage of the Rosebud battle, General Crook sent Captain Anson Mills and some soldiers to take the lead in attacking a supposed Indian camp below the canyon. But after Mills and his men had left, Crook sent word for them to come back. Captain Nickerson took the message. Nickerson explained Crook's reversal order in this way: "He cannot move out to support you, on account of his wounded."

Now, General Crook, with a force numbering 1,000 men or more, had nine men killed during the entire course of the battle, which lasted eight or nine hours. It seems reasonable to estimate that at the time the message to Mills was sent, the percentage of wounded among the Crook soldiers was not any greater, and possibly was less, than among Reno's 420 men. Yet General Crook decided he ought to stay where he was. Comparing Crook's case with Reno's, it would appear entirely excusable that Reno should have decided not to "relieve" other forces, especially when it was not known that the other forces needed relief, nor was it known just where they might be found.

The leading troops in the Reno movement toward the Custer position got to where they could see a host of Indians milling around over a ridge and its slopes. The Indians were doing much shooting, as was indicated by puffs of smoke. The air over there was seen to be filled with powder smoke and with dust kicked up by horses. It could not be seen clearly just what the Indians were doing, but no soldiers could be seen. There was general agreement in the opinion that Custer had been repulsed and had withdrawn from the field. Since his detachment was nowhere in view, the supposition was that he had gone farther away from the Reno forces.

Some Indians appeared in front of the moving Reno soldiers. Others appeared soon afterward. It was not long before all of the warrior horsemen at the distant scene were racing back to fight again against the white men approaching them. The soldiers were crowded back. The retreat was reasonably slow and in order. It was continued until the original hill position was regained. The utter impracticability of taking any other action was plainly evident to all. The general feeling was expressed by Captain Benteen in his Reno trial testimony: "A movement could have been made down the river in the direction Custer had gone, but we would all have been there yet."

Hurried preparations were made for the stand at the hilltop location. The Indians gradually surrounded the white men. The ensuing battle lasted all the remainder of that long June afternoon. At dawn the next morning, June 26, it was resumed and was kept up until late in the afternoon. Then the warriors withdrew and the vast aggregation of Indians permanently left the scene. Throughout that time of fighting—the total time in the two days amounting to about 12 to 14 hours—the soldiers exhibited a courage meriting high praise. Many of them had undergone their "baptism by fire," and the two or three hours between the original encounter and the hilltop siege afforded them time to steady their nerves. At a few times in the course of the long period of combat, there were indications of uncontrollable emotion among some, but there was no general spread of the feeling. Of the original Reno men, it may be guessed that most of those killed in the valley had been the more excitable ones. The loss on the hill that afternoon and the next day was 18 men killed and 41 or 42 wounded.

The idea of remaining on the hill where missing comrades might see them and rejoin them proved to be of vital importance to four more men. On that night of June 25, Jackson and Girard, two scouts, worked their way across the river and to the hilltop. Lieutenant DeRudio and Private Thomas O'Neil, who had also been left behind in the timber, crept along and hid, gradually moving towards the east, until they arrived among their fellows during the night of the 26th, after all the Indians had gone. All of these four men were on foot.

What would have become of these four men if the effort to go northward had been successful, or if a position far off in that direction had been established? And what would have become of Herendeen and the 11 men who joined Reno just as the pack train came to him if he had gone on northward as soon as Benteen arrived? Reno's official report, a week later, gave the valley loss as having been 29 enlisted men and three officers—including Dr. DeWolf—killed. No mention of any wounded. It is probable that not all of those men listed as "killed" were actually killed instantly.

Throughout the time of the hilltop siege fighting, there were many expressions of condemnation of Custer for having gone away, or for his having failed to send them a messenger telling them his position. But the more calm and considerate men among them held to the idea that Custer had wounded men enough to occupy him at whatever position he was holding, and that no messenger from him could get through, as messengers sent out by Reno had had to return to him. It may be that Reno and some of the officers and veteran enlisted men who had been with him in the valley fighting harbored suspicions that Custer's inexperienced men had caused him the same sort of trouble that had shattered their own efforts. But there is no record of their having given open expression to such thoughts. Apparently, nobody during the two days on the hill said anything which showed that any thought of the complete annihilation that had actually occurred had entered their minds. They learned of the catastrophe in the mid-forenoon of the 27th when the Gibbon soldiers arrived on the scene. Then the astounding and heartrending information was given to them in response to their rather petulant inquiry: "Where is Custer?"

A week or so after the Little Bighorn battle, a petition was circulated among the remaining members of the Seventh Cavalry regiment asking that Major Reno be promoted to the rank of lieutenant colonel, and that he be retained in the regiment in Custer's place. The petition was signed by 235 members of the regiment and was sent up through military channels to the highest authority. Special friends of Major Reno have pointed to this incident as indicative of his high merit. A more fitting interpretation of it would be that it showed a feeling that he did not deserve censure because of the crushing defeat, since there had been some declared opinions that he did deserve such censure. It appears that, in fact, he had few if any positive admirers as a man, but there was nevertheless no general feeling that he had failed to perform any duty incumbent upon him at any time during the battle. The petition was, however, ignored. The practice of making promotions initiated by popular petition has never been regarded as sound policy in military circles.

Throughout the entire United States there were thunderings that some individual or another was guilty of something or other that had caused the amazing reverse. In the popular thought, either Custer or Reno was the culprit. Custer was dead, so whoever blamed him could not punish him. Reno, being alive, received a great deal of abuse. From Reno's viewpoint, however, the situation did not develop beyond the point of reasonable endurance for almost two years. A hero-worshiping biographer of Custer initiated a movement for a congressional investigation of the Little Bighorn battle. He wrote a letter to W. W. Corlett, the congressional delegate from Wyoming, in which he made caustic charges concerning Reno's conduct at the Little Bighorn and intimated that Benteen also needed investigating. The letter was published on June 13, 1878. Nine days later Major Reno wrote to President Rutherford Hayes and requested that charges be brought against himself so that he might be tried by military court-martial.

The court-martial took place in January 1879. Twenty-three witnesses gave testimony. All of them had been in the battle. The judgment of the court-martial completely exonerated Reno. Whoever studies the testimony cannot rationally arrive at any conclusion other than that he did the best he could at the time of the battle, and better than many another officer might have done.

But, notwithstanding this exoneration, hosts of people continued to execrate Reno. He became a semi-outcast in social circles. Some officers in the regiment maintained only coldly formal associations with him. In general, the cold formality was based on personal dislike of him, not upon the belief that he was guilty as "the murderer of Custer," as some of his accusers called him. It also seems that his inclination to barroom brawling was aggravated by the situation in which he found himself. On one occasion something occurred that led him to make a fistfighting assault upon a fellow officer. For that offense he was court-martialed and dishonorably discharged from the army.

Reno had been a brave and capable officer in the Civil War. He had been brave and capable—or at least not craven and incapable—in the Seventh Cavalry. Possibly, his personal character was unsound. Nevertheless, there was no proper basis for the strong criticism to which he was subjected for his conduct at the battle of the Little Bighorn.

THE WHISKEY QUESTION

Among the alleged causes of the Custer tragedy is one which attributes it to drunkenness that day among officers and enlisted men. Reports of this fancied prime factor were flared in a Denver news publication not long after the battle. They were denied at once by various Seventh Cavalry survivors. Nevertheless, whisperings about these reports have persisted for many years, being circulated as a supposed secret being suppressed in deference to the feelings of Mrs. Custer. Only after her death, it was said, would the circumstances be fully revealed. General Godfrey was said to have told somebody in Washington—in confidence, of course—that immediately before the battle Custer "ordered the whiskey kegs to be opened" so that the soldiers could get themselves properly prepared for a hard fight. They then allegedly proceeded to fill themselves up.

In order to obtain from General Godfrey a firsthand reply, the author wrote to him about this allegation. Godfrey's reply, dated September 11, 1928, says:

> I never made the statement quoted in the alleged interview. The whole statement is a lie. There were no whiskey kegs with the command. The only persons I have heard of having whiskey were Major Reno and Fred Girard, Ree

interpreter. Varnum has said that Girard gave him a drink from a flask while in the valley.

In those times, regular army soldiers—officers as well as enlisted men—included a large number who used alcohol freely. But such free consumption was mainly indulged in at quiet times at military posts. On campaigns in the field, where fighting was expected or might occur, commanding officers regularly exerted whatever power they could to suppress drinking altogether, or else to restrict it to a degree of moderation. It is also natural for a desire for alcohol to be diminished by continued daily activity in the open air. But, notwithstanding the dissuading influence of commanding officers and the effect of open air activity, it is quite safe to presume that no band of soldiers went out in those days on a campaign of any kind without some of them taking along at least a small quantity of strong liquor for personal use.

John F. Finerty, the newspaper correspondent who accompanied General Crook on his campaign during that same summer of 1876, has thrown some light on the use of liquor among the soldiers. In his book *War-Path and Bivouac* (1890) there is a reference to Lieutenant Schwatka—later a North Pole explorer—being about to set out on a special courier mission for Crook. A captain delivered the order to Schwatka, then presented his canteen to the lieutenant, who fortified himself for the contemplated journey by drinking deeply to imbibe what Finerty covertly called "the elixir of life."

Not long after that incident, some additional officers arrived to join Crook. They told of the scarcity of water in the desert region they had just traversed. On account of this, "in order to quench their thirsts they had emptied their brandy flasks with true military promptitude."

But these occasions were early in the campaign, soon after they had left Fort Fetterman. By June 2, liquor had become scarce enough for Finerty to comment on the circumstance. On that day he and some companions encountered a newcomer, Lieutenant Crawford, "who treated several officers and myself to a most welcome stimulant." After the Crook battle on the Rosebud, on June 17, and after he had retreated to Goose Creek, Finerty depicts the sad situation as follows: "There was not in camp a bottle of beer, a glass of whiskey, or even a cigar." The Fourth of July celebration was terribly dull because "we had nothing but coffee wherewith to drink to the memory of George Washington."

On July 13, an army wagon train carrying supplies arrived at Crook's camp on Goose Creek, a few miles north of what is now Sheridan, Wyoming. A whiskey trader and his wagon, or wagons, accompanied the army freighters. The Finerty book records: "Some soldiers got drunk, one being a captain." And it adds: "General Crook ordered the whiskey barrels seized." It seems probable that Crook did this in order to compel sobriety. All doubts on this point would have been dispelled, however, if Finerty had told what happened to the whiskey after it had been "seized."

At the end of the Crook campaign, when his little army arrived in the Black Hills country in the fall, the officers assembled at a special social gathering, while the enlisted men celebrated in their own way. At the officer gathering there was "champagne procured from Deadwood and served in tin cups." Lively times among the enlisted men are indicated by Finerty's writing of conditions the following morning. The army was to go to Fort Laramie. In preparation, "Lieutenant Clark had to go around with a posse of soldiers and sober sufficient of the boys (black-smiths) to get our horses shod."

The situation in the Gibbon army that summer may also provide an insight into conditions prevailing in the Seventh Cavalry, which cannot have been too different. Although it is reasonable to suppose that some individuals in the Gibbon forces took small quantities of liquor with them at the time of leaving Fort Ellis on April 1, it would appear that the start was made under approximately bone-dry conditions. William H. White, a fully credible veteran of the Second Cavalry, who was with Gibbon, told the author:

> There was not a drop of liquor openly known among us, I believe. It may have been that some of the officers were smuggling a little, and possibly a few of the enlisted men, but I did not see at any time the least effect of any drinking except on an occasion in July when a trader came down the Yellowstone on a flatboat to our camp on Pease Bottom and brought a supply of Jamaica ginger for sale.

The diary of Lieutenant Bradley and also that of Matt Carroll, the freighter for Gibbon, both occasionally mention that liquor made its appearance. The diaries also mention other times when what Carroll regularly termed "wet goods" would have been comforting, but nothing of the sort could be obtained. The first entry on this subject is by Bradley, on May 23. He writes of a trader from Bozeman bringing a stock of goods to the Yellowstone and floating down this stream to the Gibbon encampment. The varieties of merchandise placed on sale are specified. Then: "Not the least acceptable was a keg of beer, reserved for the officers." The diary does not specify who did the reserving, but it seems probable that the itinerant merchant did it, to incur their favor so that there would be no hindrance to his transactions with their men.

Bradley tells of the officers having spent a very pleasant evening in disposing of the keg of beer. The mild stimulant caused their voices to break out into song and story. He concludes: "The occasion will long be remembered as one of the greenest spots in the campaign."

On May 28, the same trader brought more goods, including, according to the Bradley diary, "a limited quantity of whiskey and champagne cider." There is ground for a belief that some of this heavy liquid ammunition was preserved by the officers for future use. An occasion for such use came on June 5. The Gibbon soldiers had then moved down the Yellowstone and had set up camp about 12 miles below the mouth of the Rosebud and on the north side of the Yellowstone.

The day had been uncomfortably warm, but a balmy summer evening ensued. Nature was exhibiting her most enrapturing splendor. The officers at their supper mess were put into a cheerful mood by the agreeable environment, and they were moved to augment their cheerfulness still further. Bradley comments:

> Nor was coffee the only beverage. From the capacious recesses of secure mess-chests came forth at odd times nutmeg, lemon, sugar, Angostura bitters, champagne cider, and spiritus frumenti, from which were made rosebud cocktails, toddies, etc.

All of the exhilarating mixtures "were put where they would do the most good," according to the entry.

The next trader contact was on July 19, after the Custer battle, and while the Gibbon soldiers were again encamped at Pease Bottom. On this occasion White reported seeing one notable instance of drunkenness. Both the Bradley and Carroll diaries also tell of it. The intoxicant sold was Jamaica ginger, which was freely available. Captain Thompson, in particular, drank this inebriant to excess. The next morning he committed suicide. General Gibbon, upset by this shocking incident, put a stop to the liquor sales.

Matt Carroll's diary notes for August 17: "No sutler here, hence very dry." A few days later he wrote of the situation as being more pleasing. The August 20 entry states: "Two boats with sutler's goods arrived today."

A Good Templar lodge, an organization which promoted total abstinence, had been in existence at Fort Ellis for several years up to and including the campaign year of 1876. Its membership was exclusively of the soldiers there—the same soldiers who were with Gibbon in 1876. Major James Brisbin was in command at Fort Ellis, and both he and General Gibbon, the Montana Territory commander, did all that they could do to help the organization. It was given full control of the public assembly hall and library room at the post. Its members were favored in the issuing of passes to visit the neighboring town of Bozeman. Army transportation was provided for those occasions when members went in a body to visit the Bozeman Good Templar lodge. General Gibbon himself delivered temperance lectures, and in one instance he came from his headquarters at Fort Shaw and lectured at Fort Ellis on three successive nights.

It may be that similar temperance work was done at Fort Abraham Lincoln, the home headquarters post of the Seventh Cavalry, although the author has no certain information about this. But the probability that something of the sort was promoted there is indicated by Custer's known strong aversion to liquor.

The Seventh Cavalry regiment left Fort Abraham Lincoln on May 17. They were not paid before leaving, but the paymaster followed them and paid them their monthly wages a day or two later. This may have been Custer's way of preventing his men from buying any liquor before leaving the post, since it is improbable that many enlisted men would be given credit by the sutler there for any such purchase, as no debt of any kind could be collected by legal process from any enlisted man.

The soldiers' first opportunity to get liquor after they left on their journey came in June, first when they reached the Powder River, and later when they camped at the mouth of the Rosebud, on the south side of the Yellowstone. The steamboat *Far West*, loaded with army supplies, was there. The paymaster was on the boat, and the men were paid for the month of service just past. There were also two traders, James Coleman and John Smith, on the boat. Coleman's published recollections state that he sold liquor to the Custer men both at the mouth of the Powder River and at the mouth of the Rosebud, two or three days later. The retail price was one dollar a pint. Perhaps Custer could not prevent this, or else Terry suggested that prevention would not be prudent, or else both of them decided that the best course would be to make a concession to the drinkers.

The published recollections of Alexander Burkman, Custer's orderly during the expedition, relate that the men of the Seventh Cavalry drank freely when they were in camp at the mouth of the Rosebud. He tells that as the march was being made up the Rosebud Valley, Custer watched for signs of drunkenness, and those that exhibited them were sent back to lag in the rear in disgrace. It is presumable that those men who were drunk at that time used up their supply of whiskey, so that they had little or none left as the time of the battle approached.

Pack mules were carrying all the supplies being taken on the final march up the Rosebud and over to the Little Bighorn. Everything deemed not a necessity was omitted from these packs. The men on their horses were carrying rifles, revolvers, belt ammunition, canteens, saddlebags loaded with more ammunition, and temporary rations, with some personal belongings added. A man could not start out with much whiskey, in pint bottles, as a further burden. It was impracticable for him to put it in the regimental packs, for in the first place the packers would be held responsible for including it, and in the second place the owner would fear that somebody else would steal or confiscate it. It is probable therefore that, when it came to whiskey being taken along, each habitual drinker may have kept a pint carefully hidden somewhere on his person.

Officers could have had better opportunities for hiding liquor in the packs. But, knowing that Custer was strongly against drinking when a campaign was on, they would surely have been extremely cautious about doing anything of the kind. The punishment for an officer for any offense against military rules is usually more severe than the punishment for a similar offense given to an enlisted man, so that an officer would be taking a greater risk. His more thorough military training also renders him more likely to conform with the known wishes of his superiors. Furthermore, he has a strong incentive to keep sober and cool when a specially important duty confronts him. Finally, it may be that some of those Seventh Cavalry officers were total abstainers from liquor, and others may have been almost so.

There is evidence that there was at least one bottle of whiskey in the Reno detachment when it went into the fight. Fred Girard, a scout, had it. Colonel Varnum told Brininstool of being in the timber with Girard and Charles Reynolds, another scout, during the Reno fight in the valley. Varnum said that while they were there Reynolds manifested some anxiety, that Girard got out a pint of whiskey, and that Reynolds took a drink from the flask. (Godfrey, 52 years later, said that it was Varnum and not Reynolds who took the drink. Probably he associated Varnum's name with the incident, forgetting that he had only witnessed it.) The incident is confirmed by testimony at the subsequent court-martial trial of Reno, when Girard said: "Reynolds was depressed and wanted some whiskey. I gave him some." This incident, however, may be considered as showing, if anything, that whiskey was not plentiful there. At any rate, it is a trivial circumstance upon which to base a conclusion that there was enough whiskey consumed by the entire Seventh Cavalry to be the cause of their defeat.

But most of the accusations as to the ruinous effect of whiskey upon the conduct of the Little Bighorn battle have centered upon Major Reno. Let us therefore inquire into his case in particular.

In Volume Nine of the Montana Historical Society's publications, General Godfrey writes:

> I do not believe that any officer except Major Reno had any liquor in his possession. Major Reno had half a gallon keg he took with him in the field, but I don't believe any other officer sampled its contents.

But this statement is not altogether clarifying. Godfrey's phrase "he took with him in the field" does not specify whether the starting point meant was Fort Abraham Lincoln or the mouth of the Rosebud.

At the Reno court-martial trial, in the autumn of 1878, a civilian packer who had been in the hilltop siege in 1876, testified that Reno was drunk during the night of the 25th. The packer said he had a verbal controversy with the Major, and the Major was about to strike him when somebody interfered. He said further that Reno at that time had a whiskey bottle in one hand, that some of the whiskey splashed out, and that the odor of whiskey emanated from the officer. That was, however, at night, several hours after the time of the fighting in the valley. Drunkenness that night could not have affected Reno's conduct during the preceding afternoon.

But there was much testimony which contradicted that of the packer, some of it also going further and declaring that he himself had grossly misbehaved that night. As to Reno being drunk, various witnesses testified that, although he exhibited excitement and indecisiveness just after the retreat from the valley, none of them thought of him then as being under the influence of liquor, and none of them noted in him any indication of being intoxicated during any of the time spent on the hill. Lieutenant Edward Mathey, who had been in charge of the mule packs on the hill, testifying in the 1878 trial as to whether Reno had shown signs of drunkenness at any time during the battle period, said: "I never heard any intimation of it until last spring." Captain Benteen's testimony was of Reno's evident sobriety at all times during the hilltop period. He added some emphasis with these words: "I know there was not enough whiskey in the whole command to make him drunk." This declaration may be interpreted in two ways. Either Benteen meant that whiskey was extremely scarce there, or else he meant that it required plenty of whiskey—and more—to make Reno drunk.

Major Reno was known as being a rather heavy habitual drinker. It may appear, therefore, that half a gallon keg would not be an abundant supply for him, even during the three-day period spent in coming from the mouth of the Rosebud. A half-gallon may be thought of either as two quarts or as four pints. There are many heavy drinkers—or were in those times—who could consume four pints in three days without the least disturbance of either their physical or mental equilibrium. And there are—or used to be—many who can do better work with such a supply than they can without it. At all events, it seems ridiculous to suppose that even the hard-drinking Major Reno would take his jug from the packs and have it with him on his horse for the final dash upon the Indian camps.

Old Indians who were in the battle have, however, told of their discovery that the Custer soldiers had whiskey. Black Horse, a Cheyenne who was with the Little Wolf band following Custer up the Rosebud and on over the divide, was one of these informants of the author. He said that after the soldiers had left their camping place at Busby, the Indians found there a tin cup containing some whiskey. The published battle narrative of Wooden Leg, another old Cheyenne, tells of finding among the dead soldiers two or more canteens having whiskey in them. On the battlefield, in 1926, yet another old Cheyenne, Bobtail Horse, who had been a warrior there in 1876, pointed out to the author the very spot where he himself had found a soldier's canteen with whiskey in it. Bobtail Horse said that the canteen was about half full, that he drank all of it, and that soon afterward he vomited all of it up.

But these discoveries do not prove that any soldiers were drunk while the fighting was in progress. It is indisputable that whiskey has to be in the stomach, not in a canteen, in order to cause drunkenness. Those instances of finding canteens containing liquor may be construed as showing in each instance that the man was entirely sober when he died. The probability is that a pint, or possibly a quart, was the original quantity in the possession of each soldier who got a supply. The eager drinkers must have used their supplies up rapidly. The canteens having whiskey left in them must have belonged to the more moderate ones. Thus, it does not seem likely that, at the time of the battle, there was enough whiskey in the stomachs of the soldiers greatly to hinder their effectiveness.

Some people are ever on the alert to magnify out of proportion whatever example may be used to illustrate the pernicious effects of alcohol. So a commendable desire to persuade mankind to sobriety may be perverted into an exaggerated if not a fabricated "horrible example." It is possible that some one or another Custer soldier was under the influence of liquor at the time of the battle. But it is altogether improbable that many of them were. Considering all known conditions, the explanation that whiskey vitally influenced the conduct of the soldiers that day has too thin a basis to be given serious credence.

THE ARMS QUESTION

Many Custer battle writers have claimed that inferior and defective armament was the paramount factor in the soldier calamity at the Little Bighorn. Exhaustion of the ammunition supply has been regarded as a connected factor, or even the primary factor. Controversies between Custer partisans and Reno partisans about who caused the ruinous reverse have been toned down by agreements that, regardless of which one of those two officers was to blame, the guns surely were at fault. Furthermore, the exhaustion of the ammunition was a condition neither of the officers could have foreseen. Many emotional descriptions have been presented showing Custer's soldiers feverishly struggling in fruitless efforts to pry or pick out empty shells from rifles that would not eject them, or showing the soldiers gradually using up their cartridges until the last one was gone.

It does not seem right that both of those conditions could have existed at the same time. If a gun was defective, so that its extractor would not work well, the user of that gun would have had to stop shooting every time the extractor failed to operate. Thus, his ammunition would have been conserved. On the other hand, if any man used up his apportionment of cartridges, this would signify that his gun had been working well. Numerous statements claiming that many empty shells were observed around the bodies of dead soldiers have appeared in print. Such statements have been for the purpose of proving soldier courage, of proving that before a soldier was killed "he collected a heavy toll from them." But, if the statements be true, they utterly discredit the theory of defective guns. At any rate, there must have been no serious trouble with the gun used at any place where a large number of empty shells were found.

The armament for each soldier that day consisted of a Springfield rifle and a Colt revolver. Each man had a total of 100 rifle cartridges and 24 revolver cartridges in his belt and in the saddlebags behind his saddle. The belt held 50 rifle cartridges. The standard form of the belt had no special loops for the revolver cartridges, but some of the men attached an extra flap having such loops. They did not have their swords. These had been brought from their home post, but on the arrival at the mouth of the Powder River, where a base supply camp was established, all swords were discarded. A story is told of one lieutenant who kept his sword after leaving the base camp, but his companions kidded him so much about his act that, when they arrived at the mouth of the Rosebud, he sent the sword back with someone who was returning. So, of the various swords that have been "found on Custer battlefield," none was carried by any of the soldiers at the time of the battle.

The Seventh Cavalry rifle in 1876 was the 1873 model Springfield carbine. It was a single-shot of .45 caliber. The factory loading of each cartridge was with 55 grains of powder. The gun was 3 feet 5 inches in length and weighed 7 pounds 8 ounces. The Colt revolver was of .45 caliber and had six chambers. These were the firearms used by more than two-thirds of the United States cavalrymen at that time.

The infantry firearms during that era were the same, except that the infantry Springfield rifle had a longer barrel, and its cartridges were loaded with 75 grains of powder. The shorter cavalry gun was known as a 45-55 carbine. The longer infantry gun was known as a 45-75 "long-tom."

A third form of the 1873 model Springfield rifle was in use by civilians, but it was not used in the army. It was much heavier than the infantry Springfield. It also was of .45 caliber, but its cartridges were loaded with 120 grains of powder, and its bullet was long and heavy in proportion. Among the civilian plainsmen it was a favorite for hunting big game and was known as the "buffalo gun."

The particular defect in the arms that has been pointed to as a vital flaw handicapping the Custer soldiers was in the shell ejector of the rifle. A small clip that projected under the base rim of the shell jerked the shell out backward when the breechblock was lifted after firing. At times, when the gun became hot after close repetitions of firing, the shell clung in the barrel and the clip ripped through the rim, leaving the shell stuck in its place. It then had to be pried out with the point of a knife blade or with some similar instrument. Some shells were reloaded and used again and again. Such shells were weakened near the base so that the ejector sometimes jerked loose the base and kicked it out, leaving the remainder of the shell stuck in the barrel. In such instances, the ejector worked, but the weakened shell caused trouble. All of the cartridges used at the Little Bighorn battle, however, were of the original factory loaded type known as "fixed" ammunition. They were not reloaded ammunition. So, whatever difficulty the soldiers may have had was with the ejector clips ripping through the shell rims.

It appears, though, that this deficiency was not alleged to have been the cause of the military failure until some time after the Custer battle. The guns had already been in use in the army for three years, beginning in the spring of 1873, and during that time there had been no complaints about them. On the contrary, they were often boasted about as being the best guns then in existence. Possibly the flaw was noted, but it is probable that other guns of that time had worse flaws.

General Custer's letters to his wife in 1873, while he was on his Yellowstone expedition, tell of the wonderful qualities of "my new Springfield rifle." According to his estimates, it carried its bullets a remarkably long distance, up to 500 yards or more. One day when he shot three different antelope, the nearest one was 320 yards away. His brother Tom had a Winchester repeater. Custer wrote that the Winchester was good up to about 150 yards, but beyond that distance its effectiveness rapidly diminished. Captain Tom would steal his brother's Springfield for hunting whenever he could get it, and the General's orderly, Tuttle, would get it back and return it to the owner.

Lieutenant James Bradley, who was with Gibbon in 1876, wrote in his diary of the confidence among those soldiers, based mainly on the superior arms they had. "Armed with the splendid breechloading Springfield rifles, caliber .45," was his way of referring to that matter. He wrote his opinion that, thus armed, they could overcome any Indian village, however large it might be. It is probable that, with the kind of soldiers Gibbon had with him, they could have done so. William C. Slaper, a member of Reno's detachment, says in the Brininstool writings that "it was said to be the best equipped regiment as to horses, men, and accouterments that Uncle Sam had ever turned out."

High military authorities commended those Springfields. The Inspector General, under the date of October 9, 1876—more than three months after the Custer battle—included in his official report this comment: "It is believed that the merits of the small arms now in the hands of the cavalry and infantry are established." Under the date of October 10, 1876, Brigadier General S. V. Benet, chief of ordnance, made his annual official report. It includes this: "Modern wars must be fought with the most approved weapons, and none less perfect than the new model Springfields will satisfy our soldiers." He went on to say later in the same report:

> That a better arm than the Springfield may some day be invented is not at all improbable, and a magazine gun will no doubt be the arm of the future, but until such an one suitable for the military service has been perfected and approved a reserve stock of Springfields is a necessity.

There is no indication in those reports that any gun deficiency existed in the Custer battle, or in any other battle. In the various reports of the Custer battle—Terry to Sheridan, Sheridan to Sherman, and Sherman to the Secretary of War—there is no mention of armament deficiency. The Sherman report was at the end of 1876, six months after the Custer battle and after various other battles in which the same arms were used.

In 1873 Custer's soldiers used these Springfields in their two fights on the Yellowstone. His official report of those engagements mentions them approvingly. Crook's men used them in the Rosebud battle of 1876, in his battle of March 17, 1876, and in some other conflicts he had during that period. Miles' soldiers used them at Hanging Woman Creek, at Lame Deer, and in various other conflicts with Indians, including a long battle against the Nez Percé in 1877. If either of those officers or any of their men ever complained about their rifles, the complaint must have been a very mild one, not loud enough to be recorded.

It is probable that individual soldiers preferred some other make of rifle. But the general army feeling was that those single-shot .45-caliber Springfields were the best guns in their time, or at least in the earlier years of their time. Civilian pioneers rated them highly as hard shooters and hard kickers, depending upon how much powder was used when shells were reloaded. They were in army use about 25 years, until they were discarded, in 1898, at the beginning of the Spanish-American War. Even then, some of the first troops sent out were equipped with them.

The soldiers in the Reno fight never made public any reference to their guns not working satisfactorily during their charge toward the Indian camps or in the battle in the valley. A few of them have talked of some trouble with the ejectors during the long hours of fighting on the hill that afternoon and the next day. It appears, though, that this talk was not spontaneous complaining but was in response to inquiries, and that it was greatly exaggerated by writers to explain what happened to the Custer men. In fact, it was but an occasional trivial annoyance to those Reno Hill soldiers, as it probably was to the Custer soldiers. Any man on Reno Hill who had trouble with his gun could readily take possession of one that had been used by a dead comrade. Sergeant Edward Davern, who was there, testified at the Reno trial on this point: "It was an easy matter to borrow a carbine or a pistol on the hill. You could find one most any place." That must have been the case also among the Custer soldiers, and to a far greater degree. The guns of killed men were available for men still alive. Veteran warriors who were in the battle have told the author of only one rifle taken from the dead soldiers which had a shell stuck in its barrel. It was seized by a Sioux warrior. When he found the shell in the barrel, he considered the weapon to be of no further use, so he threw it into the Little Bighorn River.

It has been alleged that the Indians had superior arms, consisting mainly of the repeating Winchester or other repeating rifles. Much of the writing in this vein has been based on the idea that all of the warriors—every one of them—constantly "pumped their Winchesters" at the soldiers. The Winchester of that time is reputed to have been of .32 caliber and to have had a magazine for 14 cartridges. An earlier model of the rifle had been of .44 caliber, and it is claimed that some of the Indians may have had this version. A reasonable estimate of relative numbers in the Custer engagement may be put at eight warriors to one soldier. If every warrior had a 14-shot gun and every soldier had a single-shot gun, a statistician might figure that the warriors could shoot 112 bullets (14 bullets multiplied by 8 men) for each bullet shot by the soldiers.

The supposition that all, or many, of the Indians had repeating rifles, however, is not grounded in solid evidence. A theory that such guns were plentiful among the warriors is not consistent with general conditions among Indians in those times. Both the guns themselves and the ammunition for them were too expensive. A considerable number of the warriors had the 1852 model single-shot breech-loading Sharps, a rifle that had been in army use before it was replaced by the 1873 Springfield. The author has a Sharps carbine that was used by Spotted Wolf, a Cheyenne warrior chief, at the Little Bighorn battle.

The old muzzle-loading Civil War musket was the rifle most in use by the Indians of the 1876 era. The Civil War cap-and-ball revolver was also common among them. George Herendeen, a scout with the Seventh Cavalry in 1876, had been in the Little Bighorn region with a band of miner prospectors in 1874. During that time the exploring white men had two or three fights with Sioux or Cheyenne Indians. In his published story of those fights, Herendeen commented: "The Indians kept firing at us, but we were too far away for the old guns they had to do us any harm." At another place in the story he tells of one of their men having been chased by warriors close behind him. During that chase, "he got two flesh wounds from some old cap-and-ball pistol that did not lay him up."

Three different Cheyenne warriors who were veterans of the Custer battle told the author that the sole firearm they owned was a cap-and-ball revolver. They spoke of others who also had only this revolver. Wooden Leg, one of those old Cheyenne, had owned a muzzle-loading musket, which he had purchased in 1874. But he had been in the Cheyenne camp which was destroyed by Crook's soldiers on March 17, 1876. The soldiers captured his musket, so at the Little Bighorn battle he had only his cap-and-ball revolver—until he got a carbine from a dead soldier. Sergeant Ferdinand Culbertson, testifying at the Reno trial about the detachment's dash to retreat from the valley, said of the Indians: "Some of them fired pistols as we came along."

White Bull, who had been at the Custer battle, was among the Cheyenne who surrendered to General Miles in 1877. The author examined and made a·copy of a property receipt signed by Miles and issued to White Bull, dated April 23, 1877. The property mentioned in·that receipt was: "One (1) muzzle-loading percussion-cap rifle and two (2) ponies." In the spring of 1881, Miles' soldiers captured a camp of Hunkpapa Sioux, many of whom were veterans of the Custer battle. John Truscott, who was with Miles at that time, wrote of the firearms they took from those captives: "We found 40 rifles, of various makes, from a silver-plated Winchester to flintlocks." William H. White, a Second Cavalry soldier with Gibbon, arrived at the Little Bighorn scene two days after the battle. Private White was one of the men assigned to rummage among the abandoned tipis, which contained dead warriors, in order to procure tipi poles, buffalo skins, and Indian blankets that were used to make litters for carrying Reno's wounded men. White told the author: "I saw a flintlock rifle with a dead Sioux body on a scaffold. With another dead Sioux I saw two large cap-and-ball revolvers." The author has a cap-and-ball revolver that was found on the Custer field not long after the battle. Since all of the soldiers in that engagement had Colt cartridge revolvers, this cap-and-ball revolver must have belonged to some Indian.

One reason that the Indians preferred muzzle-loading firearms was that they were relatively inexpensive. Moreover, their ammunition was less expensive. The Indians got lead and molded their round bullets, which they carried in their mouth during an intensive pursuit of game. Percussion caps were carried in little boxes in a pocket. Powder was carried in powder horns or flasks. Whenever there was a shortage of powder, the Indians reduced the amount used for short distance shooting. On the other hand, if powder was plentiful, they would increase the ordinary amount so they could shoot unusually hard or an unusually long distance. They Indians liked this flexibility of the muzzle-loaders which permitted them to use one loading for a rabbit at a short distance and another for a large animal at a long distance or for an animal or a man that might be hard to kill. This feature also endeared the muzzle-loader to many old-time white frontiersmen who preferred them over all cartridge or magazine rifles.

That the Indians of that time kept themselves supplied with "the makings" for muzzle-loaders is exemplified in the writings of Captain Bourke. He was with Crook when the Cheyenne camp was destroyed on March 17, three months before the Custer battle. He wrote of the large quantities of powder found in the lodges. He went on to say: "Besides powder, there was pig-lead, with the molds for casting, metallic cartridges, and percussion caps." Similar discoveries were made at the time of the destruction of the Cheyenne tribal camp on the Red Fork of Powder River, five months after the Custer battle.

General Sheridan's official report of the Washita battle makes reference to the discovery of 535 pounds of powder and 1,050 pounds of lead in the camp. General Godfrey's account of that battle states that he had been present in August 1868, three months before the battle, and had seen "the issue of rifles, pistols, powder, caps, lead, and bullet molds to these same Cheyennes."

This sort of issue to them indicates muzzle-loading arms. But this was some years before the 1876 fighting, and so it may be regarded as too far back in time to be a reliable guide to the Indians' armament at the Little Bighorn.

The bow and arrow was still the preferred weapon for many Indians in 1876. It involved no initial outlay of money and no money for ammunition. In addition, under many conditions the bow and arrow could be used more satisfactorily than any type of gun. In a fight, an arrow could be shot without sound or smoke to reveal the location of the shooter. Veteran warriors tell of shooting many arrows during the course of the Custer battle. There was a definite reason for this. A warrior shooting a gun had to raise his head so that he could see where to aim. He thus exposed himself to view and might receive a bullet before he could shoot one. Again, when he fired a gun he disclosed exactly his location. By using a bow and arrows, a warrior could keep himself hidden at all times and still do some effective work. The arrow was aimed upward and forward in the general direction of the soldier positions. No special target was singled out, but it was expected that the arrow in its fall would stick into a man or into the back of a horse. According to the Indians, if a few horses received such arrows in their backs, they started charging about, exciting the other horses. It was this very action that contributed greatly to the horse stampede which was so disastrous for the Custer soldiers. The same thing could not have been accomplished by keeping concealed in a gully shelter and firing bullets forward and upward to fall upon the soldiers or horses. Any bullet thus shot would have been but a slight annoyance when it made a hit after its fall.

Even if a considerable number of the Indians did have Winchester or Henry repeaters, that would not have given them the great advantage alleged in explanation of their victory over Custer. In the first place, it is likely that they would have been short of cartridges for them. In the second place, the longer range of the single-shot Springfield would have offset the advantage of the repeater. As has been pointed out, Custer favored the Springfield over the Winchester in this regard. Reference may also be made to a story written in 1927 by Colonel Varnum, who had been a lieutenant with Reno. Varnum says: "As regards the range of the Winchester rifles, it was not as great as the rifles we carried. One could shoot with reasonable accuracy up to 1,000 yards with the Springfield carbine." That estimate seems to be too high for those carbines, but it may be lowered considerably and still show a great advantage over the 150 yards of reliable effectiveness that was estimated by Custer for the Winchester repeater owned by his brother. William H. White, the veteran soldier and pioneer settler in Montana, told the author: "I had a Winchester repeater, but I traded it to a Crow Indian for a single-shot Sharps carbine. I considered I made a good trade, as the Sharps would shoot much farther and harder." The Sharps gun traded for by White was the 1852 model that had been discarded by the army when the 1873 Springfield was adopted.

The fact that repeating rifles of all makes in that era were rated as being not the best for warfare is indicated by the 1876 official report of the Chief of Ordnance, which has already been quoted. He expressed the opinion that a magazine gun probably would be adopted at some later time, but that no magazine gun good enough to supplant the Springfield had yet been invented. He made it clear that rejection of the magazine guns then available was not a random decision, but that it had been carefully investigated. His view is supported by the fact that the Spencer magazine gun had been tried. It was used by the Seventh Cavalry at the Washita battle. It was displaced by the single-shot Sharps, which in turn was displaced by the single-shot Springfield.

One of the officers in the Reno battle in the valley, testifying at the Reno trial, made some statements that were plainly inconsistent and illustrated the distortions or exaggerations which have led to the supposition that the Indian armaments were superior that day. Describing the conditions when the Reno men were on their skirmish line after the halt from the original charge, he told of the hot harassment of the skirmish line soldiers by Indians "pumping their Winchesters." He went on to tell of the warriors shifting gradually to the soldiers' left. He stated that the Indian ponies were kicking up much dust, which obscured the view of the warriors, and he estimated that they were from 800 to 1,000 yards away. It is questionable how he could say with confidence that they were "pumping Winchesters" just then. But, even if they were, those Winchester bullets would have fallen to the ground far short of the estimated distance. If the Indians were anywhere near that far away, it may be assumed that the few hits they made during the skirmish line period were by bullets from their single-shot Sharps or, more likely, from their old style muzzle-loaders prepared with unusually heavy charges of powder.

The Colt revolver of that era could shoot almost as far as its contemporary Winchester magazine rifle. As a matter of fact, in general the Colt revolver was the superior of the two, and that particular model of the Colt continued in use long after that model of the Winchester had been supplanted by better repeaters. Practically every man in the Seventh Cavalry had one of those highly efficient Colt revolvers. There were a few Remington revolvers then in army use, and some were used at the Little Bighorn, especially by civilians present or by officers who preferred the Remington. Occasional remarks in reminiscences by soldiers as well as in the Reno trial testimony intimate that some of the officers and civilians carried two revolvers. Such instances, however, were not sufficient in number to affect materially the conception of one revolver for each soldier.

It is not improbable that the total number of revolvers carried by the men in Custer's detachment exceeded the total number of Winchester or other magazine guns carried by the Indians surrounding them. The Indians' ammunition supply for the repeating rifles is a matter of even greater conjecture than the number of rifles. Each soldier had an immediate supply of 18 cartridges, 6 in the chambers and 12 in the belt. The long range of the Springfield carbines should have kept the Indians at such a distance that their magazine repeaters were ineffective. If they did get close enough to "pump their Winchesters," the soldiers could "pump their Colts" with an equal degree of damaging effect.

Some unusually long-range rifles were said to have been used by the Indians during the two days of fighting against the Reno and Benteen troops on their hilltop position. One Seventh Cavalry narrator said: "One Indian did particularly deadly work with a buffalo gun until Sergeant John Ryan spotted him, and after a shot or two the Indian sharpshooter was silenced." Ryan was mentioned as carrying a "sporting rifle" of some special make—it may have been one of the long-range buffalo guns. Colonel Varnum's story mentions that he "borrowed a long-range rifle" at a certain stage of the hilltop fighting when he wanted to make an effective shot at a particular Indian.

The infantry long-tom Springfields had a longer range than the cavalry carbine Springfields. As pointed out earlier, the infantry model was the same as the cavalry model, except that the infantry weapon had a longer barrel and used shells having longer bullets and more grains of powder. Some, and perhaps all, of the Arikara Indian scouts with the Seventh Cavalry that day had the infantry Springfields. It is not improbable that some of the accompanying civilians also had them or some other special rifles or revolvers. One or another officer may have had either a rifle or a revolver different from the army issue. For example, Captain Thomas B.

French had an infantry long-tom. Some may have carried the very large Springfield that regularly had 120 grains of powder in its cartridge and slung a very heavy bullet, or they may have had some other make of buffalo gun. But it is unlikely that many of the non-issue firearms were carried since all of the cartridges that were brought along in the army supply were for the Springfield carbines and the Colt revolvers.

The Indians fighting Reno on the hill may have had a few long-range rifles, particularly the infantry Springfields. They had killed three Arikara scouts during the first fighting in the valley and had taken their guns. They may have taken a few special guns, either rifles or revolvers, from the dead Custer men and used them in fighting Reno on the hill. In Lieutenant Bradley's diary of the Gibbon movements that summer he tells of the killing of three of their men by Indians on May 23. His diary record says: "The Indians carried off one infantry rifle and two carbines." It is probable that they obtained a few army guns at the time of the Crook battle on June 17, and possibly they got an occasional one at other times.

It is not probable that any Indian had any one of the very heavy rifles known among white men as the buffalo gun. It is possible that one or more of these guns had been taken from the Custer men or had been obtained at some earlier time. But such guns were not desired by Indians. The gun itself was too heavy to suit the Indian style of hunting, and its ammunition was too expensive. The claim that various Indians in the encirclement about Reno Hill had such rifles is supposed to have been corroborated by statements of the Indians themselves. Different Indians have told interviewers that they had "buffalo guns." But such statements have to be interpreted in accord with Indian meaning, and their conception of a buffalo gun was different from the white man's.

The white buffalo hunter rode out and located a herd. Then he dismounted and crept toward the animals. Commonly, he got down prone on the ground. Taking careful aim, he shot a buffalo. The herd was startled, but the man could not be seen, so they did not run away. They merely milled around in the same vicinity. The hunter took aim again and dropped another buffalo. The animals continued to mill around. The hunter shot one after another, usually for some time. In this way, white hunters regularly made a big killing, often almost cleaning up a small herd. In order that the hunter might keep himself as far as possible out of the sight and scent of the herd, and so that he might send killing bullets across the long intervening distance, he used the heaviest and hardest shooting rifle he could obtain. Since he commonly shot from a prone position, the weight of such a gun was not too great an inconvenience.

Besides the heavy Springfield, there was a heavy Sharps, and there may have been other heavy models made especially for the buffalo hunters or for similar use. Bechdoldt, writing of buffalo hunters south of the Arkansas River in 1874, says they were armed with long barreled single-shot Sharps rifles of .50 caliber. Another writer mentions that the weight of the Sharps buffalo gun was "more than 20 pounds." He tells of the high cost of ammunition for it. He also says that its barrel would heat up after two or three closely successive shots so that it had to be cooled in order to prevent distortion of the barrel from overheating. A veteran Fort Ellis cavalryman told the author of a certain Lieutenant Doane who had one of those heavy Sharps in 1875. According to the veteran, it was of .50 caliber and its bullets would carry up to 1,500 yards.

Those various unusually heavy rifles were what white men had in mind when they spoke of buffalo guns. The Indian idea of a buffalo gun was of one that was unusually light in weight. This was because the Indian way of hunting buffalo was quite different from the white man's way.

The Indian buffalo hunter rode his pony right into the herd. As the herd set off running, the Indian guided his pony to follow a certain animal. Riding up from behind and to the side of the big game animal, the Indian sent an arrow or a bullet into its chest. He repeated this action until the buffalo began to stumble and to bleed at the nostrils. Then the hunter left the animal to fall and die slowly, while he centered his attention upon another one, which he dealt with in like manner. When he was using a gun instead of his bow and arrows, the Indian hunter wanted a lightweight gun that could be carried conveniently while he was bareback on his running pony. If it was a gun he could fire one-handed, it was even better. The old cap-and-ball revolvers were well suited to this way of killing buffalo. The shortest and lightest rifles could be used. But, in order to improve the firearm for shooting into the vital parts of a running buffalo, the Indian sawed off the rifle barrel to a shorter length, and sometimes he sawed off the butt. That was the perfect buffalo gun of the Indian. That was what the Indian had in mind when he told the untutored

interviewer that he had "a buffalo gun" for fighting the Seventh
Cavalry soldiers. It is possible, too, that he had in mind some
other lightweight rifle or a cap-and-ball revolver.

The marksmanship of the average Indian with a rifle or other
firearm was distinctly inferior to that of the average white man.
It is true that some of those Seventh Cavalry soldiers were inexperienced in rifle shooting, but it is not improbable that even
the inexperienced ones could shoot as well as or better than the
average warrior pitted against them. Practically every Indian who
had a rifle carried with it a forked stick to use as a gun rest when
taking aim. Rarely did an Indian ever try to hold the rifle out
forward and shoot without a rest, as white men regularly did.

When Indians were enlisted as soldiers, during the times following the Indian wars era, their poor marksmanship became notorious. Even after long practice under capable teaching, they were
not able to match the marksmanship of the white soldiers. Under
conditions in which the average white soldier could put his bullet
at or in the immediate vicinity of the center of a target, the average
Indian would miss the target board entirely. He could more
closely match the white man when a revolver was used or when
the shooting was done at a moving target. So, a rifle that would
carry its bullets a long distance was not especially useful to an
Indian. His inability to shoot straight at short distances would
simply be amplified over long distances.

The rifles and revolvers taken from the Reno men killed in the
valley were undoubtedly used in fighting the Custer soldiers.
There probably were 25 to 30 of each kind of weapon. It may be
estimated that an even greater number of Reno's horses were
left behind there—killed, wounded, or abandoned in the flight.
Each horse carried extra ammunition in saddlebags. This ammunition was available for use in the guns taken by the Indians. So,
in the warrior ranks around the Custer soldiers there were 25 to 30
Indians who had Springfield carbines. A few of those guns may
have been infantry long-toms. The warriors also had the 25 or 30
Colt revolvers they had taken. For those newly acquired weapons
the Indians had whatever cartridges they got from the belts of
the dead Reno soldiers and from the saddlebags on their horses.
It is altogether likely that the warriors who had those Reno guns
and ammunition were the best armed warriors around the Custer
men. But it is also altogether likely that the Custer men were
by far the better at using those arms.

The idea that the Indian victory over Custer resulted from the
superiority of Indian armament arose from stories of members

of the Seventh Cavalry who fought those Indians the remainder of that afternoon and the next day on the hill, and from later elaborations of these stories by imaginative writers. During that long period of fighting, however, those soldiers did not know what had happened to the Custer detachment. They did not know that the warriors besieging the hilltop position were armed with about 213 rifles and 213 Colt revolvers taken from Custer's dead soldiers, in addition to the 25 or 30 rifles and revolvers taken from the Reno men in the valley, and that they had plenty of ammunition for all of them.

Those were the "superior arms" mistakenly reputed to have been in the possession of the Indians during the weeks alleged to have been spent in preparation for the coming of the Seventh Cavalry. According to statements of veteran warriors who were there, those soldier guns were prized as the best of guns. Dr. Joseph K. Dixon, in his *The Vanishing Race: Last Great Indian Council* (1913), quotes Runs-the-Enemy, a Sioux, as saying: "The guns and ammunition that we gathered from the dead soldiers of Custer's command put us in better fighting condition than ever before." Various other former warriors have been quoted in a similar vein, and there has been no expression to the contrary. More than a score of former warriors have responded to the author's inquiries about the soldier guns with the emphatic reply: "Good gun, heap good gun."

Although a few of the soldiers who had been in the hilltop battle persisted for a long time in declaring that the original guns of the Indians were superior, they eventually toned down their declarations or decided they had been mistaken. Colonel Varnum, after 50 years of pondering over the matter, greatly modified the opinions he had expressed soon after the battle. In his story published in 1927, he concludes: "In regard to the guns used by the Indians against us, I believe the longest range rifles they had were those they had taken from General Custer's command, with some few exceptions." The final phrase—"with some few exceptions"—is merely a polite way of refraining from contradicting others who might continue to maintain the views declared in past times.

Bows and arrows have a prominent place in the talk of veteran warriors discussing their fight against the Custer men. This is the case, however, only when their talk is spontaneous and is not prompted by the questions of a white man that lead them out of their natural channels of reflective thought. But they do not talk spontaneously of bows and arrows in discussing the fight against

the Reno men on the hilltop. There is corroboration for this discrepancy. Thousands of arrows were found in the bodies of the
dead men and horses on Custer field. Although many of them
were imbedded thus after death had occurred, it is likely that a
considerable number of them were hits in the course of the battle.
In contrast, none of the men on Reno Hill ever talked of arrows
being shot at them. Taking these various elements into consideration, it appears that the Indians used bows and arrows when
fighting Custer because they lacked good firearms. Then, with
plenty of good guns and cartridges obtained from Custer and his
men, there was no need for much use of bows and arrows in the
subsequent fighting against the Reno soldiers on the hilltop.

There is also a vital flaw in the theory that the Custer soldiers
exhausted their ammunition supply. Each soldier began the battle
with a total of 50 rifle cartridges and 18 revolver cartridges in his
weapons and in his belt. In addition, each horse carried saddlebags containing 50 rifle cartridges and probably some additional
revolver cartridges. A clue to the rate of their use may be gathered
from statements of Reno combatants. Lieutenant Charles De-
Rudio, testifying about the valley fight, stated: "I fired 21 shots,
but some of the men told me they fired 60." Lieutenant George
Wallace estimated that the number of cartridges used averaged
40 per man. Neither of these officers specified any distinction
between rifle and revolver cartridges.

But there was a difference in the conditions of the Reno fighting
in the valley and the Custer fighting on his ridge. The Reno men
were moving almost constantly, and they had little opportunity
to take either guns or cartridges from their killed men or horses.
The Custer men were, supposedly, settled at fixed locations and
were waging a pitched battle. So, both dead men and dead horses
were at hand, and guns and ammunition could be promptly taken.

The original supply of each individual was diminished, of
course, as the battle proceeded. But, both guns and ammunition
could be confiscated from the dead men. If the deaths were oc-
curring in gradual course, as should have been the case, it is conceivable that the diminishing group of resisters had many more
cartridges and guns than they could use. All of this reasoning is
applicable only if the soldiers were remaining at their posts.

Cartridges were in the belts taken from the dead soldiers by
the Indians. In some instances only a few were gone; in other
instances one-third or one-half or more were gone. In no instance,
according to veteran informants of the author, were all gone. Red
Horse, a veteran Sioux warrior, has been quoted as saying: "I

took a gun and two belts off two dead soldiers. Out of one belt two cartridges were gone, out of the other five."

The stampeded horses took away much reserve ammunition in the saddlebags. But the observers on the battlefield three days after the fight found 70 dead horses that had been soldier mounts. It is probable that, in most of those instances, the soldiers got the ammunition from the saddlebags. It can be believed that most of those horses were intentionally killed by the soldiers, to be used as breastworks. According to the Indian estimates, the general horse stampede did not take place until after about an hour and a half of fighting. The fact that the warriors then found plenty of ammunition in those saddlebags indicates that there had been no shortage up to that time.

It appears, then, that the Custer soldiers were neither out of ammunition nor handicapped because of a lack of well functioning guns. It must have been that whatever good fighting they had been doing was changed into a rampant confusion by the stampeded horses charging helter-skelter among them. Then, as the veteran warrior recountings express the situation, they became a band of white men suddenly "gone crazy."

OTHER BATTLES
WITH THE INDIANS

For purposes of comparison with the catastrophe at the Little Bighorn, some other battles with Indians may be briefly reviewed. The particular items that will be noted in each instance are the numbers of whites and Indians involved, the number of white fatalities, the armament, and any other pertinent conditions. A study of these battles may help establish what should have been the outcome of the Custer battle if Custer's soldiers had fought as those other men did. For this review, selection has been made of battles fought under conditions somewhat similar to those of the Custer battle. The differences are mainly in magnitude, not in general character.

The Hayfield Fight occurred on August 1, 1867. Its scene was the valley of the Bighorn River a few miles below Fort C. F. Smith. About half a dozen civilian workmen were cutting hay there to supply the post. A detachment of 19 soldiers from the post were camped with the workmen as a military guard. Lieutenant Sigismund Sternberg was in command of the soldier guards. On that first day of August, an outpost picket guard fired a shot as a notice that he saw Indians lurking near at hand. The hayfield workmen rushed to the camp center and into a brush corral that had already been prepared as a frail defensive shelter.

The soldiers also assembled there. The civilian workmen were all armed, so the defensive force may be considered as consisting of 25 men.

The Indians at once surrounded the brush corral. Some of the area within gunshot distance around the corral was open, but much of it had plum thickets, chokecherry trees, and other wild shrubbery which afforded hiding places for the warriors. The number of warriors has been estimated by white men involved as being from 200 to 500. The Indians thus outnumbered the whites by somewhere between 8 to 1 and 20 to 1. According to F. G. Burnett, a civilian participant, the battle was waged from 9 A.M. to 6 P.M. Three white men were killed—Lieutenant Sternberg and two enlisted men. The Indian death loss was estimated in the excessively high figures commonly claimed in such cases.

The soldiers were using the single-shot breech-loading Springfield rifles of .50 caliber. Each one also had a Colt revolver. One of the civilians had an old Enfield muzzle-loading musket, while the others had Spencer or Henry magazine rifles. They probably also had revolvers. It appears that they all had plenty of cartridges, as their stories make no reference to a shortage of ammunition. The Indians probably had a mixture of guns along with bows and arrows, as was usual with them. The whites certainly had the better arms. The fact that they fought through nine hours and lost only 3 men out of 25—a loss of 12 percent—indicates that they held their ground bravely. The white men claimed to have killed between 50 and 100 warriors, while the Indians claimed that only a single warrior was killed.

The Wagon Box Fight took place near Fort Phil Kearny on August 2, 1867, the day after the Hayfield Fight. Some civilian employees were getting lumber and fuel to supply the post. A company of infantrymen, led by Captain James Powell and Lieutenant John C. Jenness, were camped with them as guards against Oglala Sioux raiders who were constantly harassing all the whites around Fort Phil Kearny. At the soldiers' camp 14 wagon boxes were placed end-to-end on the ground in an elliptical loop enclosing a corral.

When the Indians were seen coming at about 7 A.M., all of the soldiers and a few of the civilians got into the wagon boxes. There were 32 white men involved. The soldiers had the same model Springfield rifles and Colt revolvers used by the Fort C. F. Smith soldiers in the Hayfield Fight. One civilian had a Spencer repeating rifle, which was faster but weaker than the Springfield. The other civilians had rifles of some kind, and each civilian undoubtedly also had a revolver. The diary of R. J. Smith, one of the civilians, says he had two Colt revolvers. All of the white men participants reported that their arms were better than those of the Indians. They were speaking primarily of their .50-caliber single-shot breech-loading Springfields. Sergeant Gibson recounted that his Springfield made an effective shot at 700 yards.

Six different charges were made by the Indians during about six hours of fighting. Most of the charging was by horsemen. They dashed forward very close to the thin board barricades and then swerved away and returned to their starting points. This was the standard Indian style of making charges. Arrows carrying firebrands started some fires in the animal litter of the enclosed corral. The besieged white men were relieved by the arrival of other soldiers from Fort Phil Kearny, which was about six or seven miles away. They brought with them a Howitzer cannon, and fired it as they approached. This caused the Indians hurriedly to complete a retreat they had already begun. The end of the fighting was at about 1 P.M.

Lieutenant Jenness and Privates Haggerty and Doyle were killed. The number of warriors in that fight has been estimated at figures ranging from 400 to 3,000. So, the warriors outnumbered the white men by between 13 to 1 and 100 to 1. Approximately ten percent of the white men were killed. Even though suicidal preparations were made, as will be shown later, those 32 men carried on a brave battle against heavy odds for a long time.

The Battle of Beecher Island took place on September 17-19, 1868. Its site was on a branch of the Arikaree River, in northeastern Colorado. General George A. Forsythe was in command of 50 civilian volunteers. They were hunters, trappers, or other frontiersmen. Many of them were veteran volunteer soldiers of the Civil War. Forsythe got 30 of them from around Fort Harker and 20 from around Fort Hays, both of which were in Kansas. Since they were civilians, not soldiers, each man probably had his personal preference as to arms. It appears, though, that most of them had Spencer magazine rifles and Colt revolvers.

The Indians around the Forsythe men were Cheyenne. Their estimated number is commonly fixed at about 500. The battle was carried on through a large part of September 17. The Indians remained in the vicinity and renewed their attacks on the subsequent two days. The distress of the white men all through the first day was severe, and the additional attacks on the following days made the distress a very long one. The "island" was not much more than a sandbar projecting out into a riverbed that was just then almost dry, so the Indians had little difficulty getting as close as they wanted to the white men's position.

Four men were killed, including the surgeon, Dr. Moers. Nine men, including General Forsythe, were seriously wounded. Eight others received wounds in lesser degrees. Thus, almost half of the men were hit. If the estimate of 500 Indians is accepted—although it is probably too high, as such estimates regularly are—the Indians outnumbered the whites during those three days of fighting by ten to one. The four men killed constitute a loss of eight percent. Although thoughts of suicide must have been in the minds of those besieged men, they do not make mention of it in their accounts. Surely, they waged a brave fight.

In September 1873, there was a pitched battle for two days in Utah between white men and Ute Indians. One troop of soldiers and a body of civilians were encircled by the warriors during that long period. Eleven civilians, three officers, and two enlisted men were killed. The Indians finally withdrew and left the remaining white men as victors.

A noted frontier battle occurred at Adobe Walls, a trading post near the Canadian River in Hutchinson County, Texas, on June 27, 1874. The 28 white men involved were buffalo hunters, and one woman was with them. Various Indian tribes in that region south of the Arkansas were upset by the white intrusion upon hunting grounds which at that time were reserved by treaty for Indians only. A great joint war party of Cheyenne, Apache, Comanche, and probably some Kiowa was organized to drive out the band of hunters. Estimates about the number of Indians engaging in the battle are quite vague, although a combined total of 500 warriors seems low enough. Their attack was planned beforehand, and they "made medicine" to their satisfaction in preparation for it. It may thus be supposed that they tried their best to kill those white men.

The battle lasted six or seven hours, from early morning until sometime after noon. Three white men, or a little more than ten percent of their number, were killed. The white men had an important advantage insofar as they had some remnant adobe buildings for barricades. Nevertheless, their fighting through six or seven hours and their driving away prepared warriors who outnumbered them almost 20 to 1 shows what white men normally could do when surrounded by Indians, if the white men maintained unshaken determination.

The Fetterman Fight, which occurred on December 20, 1866,

offers the closest similarity to the Custer battle insofar as all of the soldiers were killed. Oglala Sioux, with occasional help from the Cheyenne, had been threatening Fort Phil Kearny every day since the fort had been established in July 1866. On that December day, a small band of warriors attacked a train of wagons carting wood two or three miles from the post. Captains W. J. Fetterman and Frederick H. Brown led 81 soldiers out to drive away the warriors. The Indians fled and the soldiers followed. They all disappeared over a ridge and out of sight from the lookout points of the post. Firing was heard beyond the ridge, and additional soldiers were sent out. When the additional soldiers arrived, they found every one of the preceding white men dead. Several hundred warriors were lingering in view in the distance, making challenging gestures.

The warriors who fought the Fetterman-Brown men were the same Oglala Sioux who had been annoying the men at Fort Phil Kearny for several months and who later fought the 32 men in the Wagon Box Fight. It is probable that approximately the same number of Indians were in the two engagements. But the fighting of the white men was utterly different in the two instances. General Henry B. Carrington, commander of Fort Phil Kearny in 1866, later gave an estimate of the duration of the Fetterman-Brown encounter. Speaking at the unveiling of a monument on that battle ridge in 1908, he said: "The whole firing was over and the last man was killed inside of 21 minutes." This 100 percent loss of the 83 men in 21 minutes is in strong contrast with the 10 percent loss of the 32 men in 6 hours at the Wagon Box Fight. Such a tremendous discrepancy needs an explanation.

The United States Senate appointed a commission to inquire into this tragic affair. The commission was composed of four generals of the army and two civilians. They took testimony, examined the case thoroughly, and made a report. The report tells of the dead bodies of Fetterman, Brown, and 65 of their followers having been found "in a space not exceeding 30 feet in diameter." It says that "at this point there were no indications of a severe struggle." As an indication of the fact that there had been no soldier resistance there, the report states: "No empty cartridge shells were about, and there were some full cartridges."

A different aspect was presented at another area some distance from the nonresisting men. The commission's report says that at this other area the bodies of Lieutenant G. W. Grummond, four or five soldiers, and three civilians were found. The report particularizes those four or five soldiers as "old and experienced soldiers." Many empty cartridge shells were found with this group, and various blood pools and ten dead Indian ponies nearby showed that they had fought well. The report emphasizes this conclusion by adding: "No Indian ponies nor pools of blood were found at any other point."

Those eight or nine men evidently did the only genuine determined fighting that was done during the 21 minutes of battle. They were included in the 100 percent loss. They might have held their ground longer, until reinforcements came, if the other white men had not been present at the beginning. The nonresistance of those other men must have powerfully disheartened the nine and, on the other hand, encouraged the Indians, making them more bold. The total massacre was not a case of an insufficient number of men. It was a case of too many men.

Although there was universal agreement in expressed opinions that Fetterman and Brown committed suicide, there was no open statement of belief that any of the other men had done so. A study of all of the accounts and comments discloses a strained effort not to make any such statement. The reticence was probably motivated by a desire not to harm the morale of the United States Army in general. The post's surgeon is said to have expressed an opinion that all but six of the men had been killed not by bullets, but by arrows or other weapons. This seems highly improbable. All observers of the bodies state that they were extensively mangled. This would render it impracticable to discover which wound was the fatal one, or whether or not there was a bullet hole concealed among the gashings and smashings of heads and bodies. In 1908, one Fort Phil Kearny soldier veteran allowed his tongue to slip, and he expressed his true thoughts. In a talk at the unveiling of the monument, he spoke of "the spot where they gave up their lives, probably self-inflicted, after all hope was gone." But why would all hope have been gone after only 21 minutes?

Red Cloud and other Oglala Sioux who took part in that whirlwind affair talked of it afterward to Captain James Cook, who resided for many years near their Pine Ridge Agency in South Dakota. Cook says they told him that the white soldiers seemed paralyzed, offered no resistance, and were simply knocked in the head. Old Northern Cheyenne Indians who were there have talked of it to the author. They say that Crazy Mule, a noted Cheyenne worker of magic, performed one of his miracles on that occasion. He caused the soldiers to become dizzy and bewildered, to run aimlessly here or there, to drop their guns, and to fall dead.

Crook's battle on the Rosebud, eight days before the Custer battle, was against the same Indians who fought Custer. The Crook battle was carried on through the better part of a day, lasting perhaps eight or nine hours. Nine of his soldiers were killed. But Crook had a large force of men, and the Indians outnumbered them only about three to one, as compared with the ten to one ratio in the case of Custer. The incidents are thus similar only insofar as the Indians and the armaments that were used were the same. The great contrast is that Crook lost only nine men while Custer lost all of his men, and that Crook fought eight or nine hours while Custer fought an hour and a half or a little longer.

The Reno battle on the hilltop can also be compared with the Custer battle. The same warriors fought in the two cases. It is true that Reno had 412 men while Custer had 213. But the numerical advantage was offset by the fact that, when the Indians were around Reno, they had all of the Custer guns and much of his ammunition in addition to what they had while fighting the Custer soldiers. The stories told by Reno veterans about hard fighting on the part of the Indians are entirely believable, although this does not necessarily mean that they fought equally hard against Custer. The great difference between the two cases lies in the duration of the fighting and in the losses sustained. Over the two days, the Reno hilltop fighting lasted about 14 hours, during which time the loss was 18 men, or about four percent of the forces.

The Reno men on the hilltop had an advantage insofar as they had two or more hours of warning about the number of Indians in the camps, and they were able to assemble themselves with better composure to resist the onslaughts when the Indians attacked them. The Custer men probably had no more than 15 to 30 minutes in which to learn about the unexpectedly great number of warriors who would meet them. They were still on their horses moving forward when they obtained this information, and the dismounting and beginning of the battle followed quickly. Their complete encirclement took place soon thereafter. This must have been an important factor in creating mental agitation, as it undoubtedly was in the Fetterman-Brown case.

The Custer men were probably discouraged by the fact that

Reno and Benteen did not come to their aid. On the other hand, the Reno men on the hilltop expected Custer to come and help them. When he did not do so, they were troubled by thoughts of having to do all the fighting by themselves. They were further disturbed by thoughts that he might have been defeated or that he had withdrawn from a battle he considered he could not win. Although, on the whole, those men on the hilltop fought well, there were some indications of extreme discouragement, some inklings that they might have gone into a panic if their situation had been precisely as that of the Custer men. Captain Benteen's story, as published by Brininstool, relates that he had a good deal of trouble keeping his men on the line.

General Godfrey wrote of a strange incident in connection with a countercharge against the Indians made by Benteen's men on the hilltop. One man who belonged in the charging group stayed hidden in an entrenchment pit. The charge was successful. The Indians scurried away, and none of the soldiers received the slightest scratch. The man who stayed in the pit had been "crying like a child," according to Godfrey. He went on to say: "Directly after everyone had gotten into the pits again the one man who did not go was shot in the head and killed instantly." That is strange. He was in the pit "crying like a child." Supposedly, he was where Indian bullets could not hit him, and yet the man "was shot in the head and killed instantly." The question arises, who fired that shot?

Many instances all through our pioneer and Indian frontier history could be reviewed to show that effective fighting was done by small numbers of white men surrounded by large numbers of Indians, when—as was regularly the case—the white men fought resolutely, and kept right on fighting resolutely. The multitude of such instances makes it impracticable to discuss all of them. The few just reviewed may serve to exemplify hundreds of others.

A summary of the key points in the battles reviewed follows:

Hayfield Fight—men engaged, 25; outnumbered, between 8 and 20 to 1; death loss, 12 percent in 9 hours.

Wagon Box Fight—men engaged, 32; outnumbered, 13 to 1, possibly much more; death loss, 10 percent in 6 hours.

Beecher Island—men engaged, 50; outnumbered, 10 to 1; death loss, 8 percent in 16 or more hours on 3 successive days.

Adobe Walls—men engaged, 28; outnumbered, about 20 to 1; death loss, 10 percent in 6 or 7 hours.

Fetterman Fight—men engaged, 83; outnumbered, probably about 10 to 1; death loss, 100 percent in 21 minutes.

Reno Hill—men engaged, 412; outnumbered, 5 to 1; death loss, 4 percent in about 14 hours on 2 successive days.

Crook's battle—men engaged, about 700; outnumbered, almost 3 to 1; death loss, slightly more than 1 percent in 8 or 9 hours.

Custer battle—men engaged, 213; outnumbered, 10 to 1; death loss, 100 percent in less than 2 hours.

In all of those other battles, with the exception of Reno Hill and Crook, the ratio of Indians to whites was at least as high as the ratio in the Custer battle. In all except the Fetterman incident the battle duration was much longer than the Custer battle. Nevertheless, the Custer loss was 100 percent, while the others —except in the Fetterman instance—ranged from slightly more than 1 percent to 12 percent. No white man was left to tell why the Custer battle was a complete failure. The Indians never have understood just how it came about. The question can be answered only by a full analysis of all pertinent circumstances in the entire case.

THE INDIAN TESTIMONY

Veteran warriors from among the Northern Cheyenne have been the author's chief source of Indian information about the Custer battle. They can be considered to be the best Indian informants for the following reasons:

First, the Cheyenne had occupied the Little Bighorn region for 20 or more years before the Custer battle, after having wrested it from the Crow. On various occasions in preceding years, the Cheyenne tribal camp had been set up on the very spot where it was standing when the Custer soldiers came. So, they knew thoroughly the surrounding country. On the other hand, none of the Sioux, except some of the Oglala, were acquainted with the Little Bighorn region until they arrived there with the Cheyenne a few days before the battle.

Second, the approach of the Custer detachment was at the northern end of the great group of Indian camps, where the Cheyenne camp circle was located. Therefore, according to Indian custom, it was assumed that the Cheyenne were the special target of Custer, and it was their business to take the lead in active resistance. The Oglala Sioux camp circle was next to that of the Cheyenne. This contiguity had existed at all of the preceding camping places during the movements of the combined tribes that spring. These two tribes had been warfare allies since the days of fighting near Fort Phil Kearny and Fort C. F. Smith in the period from 1866 to 1868 The Oglala warriors joined the Cheyenne to intervene between Custer and the camps. Although warriors thronged out from the Sans Arcs, Brulé, Minneconjou, Hunkpapa, and minor groups, they rode on beyond and around to the rear of the soldiers. The main body of the Cheyenne and Oglala kept their post between the soldiers and the river. The Indian camps were behind them on the other side of the river. Indeed, the Indians generally regarded that particular engagement with the Custer detachment as a battle between the Cheyenne and the soldiers, with the Oglala serving as special allies of the Cheyenne, and with warriors from all the other tribes in the great camp providing a certain amount of help.

Third, following this battle and after the campaign was ended, the Indians were driven back to the Dakota reservations. All of the Sioux tribes were permanently settled in the Dakotas. The Northern Cheyenne were settled permanently on their present reservation in Montana. The western border of their reservation is only 19 miles east of the present monument on Custer battlefield. So the Sioux, not well acquainted with the Little Bighorn scene before the battle, had no opportunity to get acquainted with it after the battle, while the Cheyenne, at home there through many years before that time, have dwelt adjacent to it ever since then. In their journeys off the reservation they often have passed the scene of the great battle and the places where, in the past, they hunted and camped. Thus, their memories have been kept constantly refreshed.

Fourth, the author served as a doctor on the Northern Cheyenne Reservation from 1922 to 1926 and subsequently moved to the Crow Reservation within which the Custer battlefield is located. He has thus had the opportunity to know various veteran Cheyenne warriors. They have accompanied him to the battlefield area, pointed out precise spots of special interest, and described salient features of the stirring event in its entirety.

Fifth, in recent years these Northern Cheyenne have been observing June 25 as an anniversary. Each of their annual tribal thanksgiving and prayer ceremonies, known to us as the Sun Dance, has included this date on which, in 1876, the Indians won a great battle.

It must be pointed out, however, that while the Cheyenne are the best Custer battle informants, there is no essential conflict between their stories and those of the Sioux.

Dr. Thomas B. Marquis speaking sign language with Turkey Leg, a veteran Northern Cheyenne warrior. (Smithsonian Institution)

The Custer soldiers were seen first by the Cheyenne, whose camp was at the north end of the group, at a point where there was an unobstructed view of the distant hills to the east. The ridge where the soldiers were first seen is more than two miles away from the Cheyenne campsite. A few Cheyenne warriors had gone to the south end of the camp group, where the Reno soldiers had approached the Hunkpapa campsite. Many warriors from all of the other camps had also converged there. But that was regarded as primarily an affair of the Hunkpapa, who guarded that end of the camps.

The Cheyenne dog soldiers—the special guards of the Cheyenne camp—crossed the river to stop the advance of the Custer soldiers toward the camp. As was explained earlier, the dog soldiers were special camp policemen appointed from time to time from one or another of the various warrior societies. On that day the Cheyenne camp policemen were of the Fox warrior society. Last Bull was their leading warrior chief. So, it was Last Bull and his immediate warrior comrades who went out first. Others followed. It was not long before practically all of the warriors from all of the camps had joined in and had surrounded the Custer soldiers on a ridge near the river. There the fighting began as a pitched battle.

The soldiers dismounted and arrayed themselves along the ridge for about a half a mile. Although all of the warriors rode out on their ponies, they dismounted and left the ponies, either picketing them by lariat to bunches of sagebrush or allowing them to go loose. The soldiers stretched out flat upon the ground. The warriors hid themselves in gulches or crept along gullies and behind little knolls and clumps of sagebrush. The Cheyenne dog soldiers and most of the other Cheyenne warriors were between the soldiers and the river, along the fence that now encloses the lower parts of the battlefield. They took this position as the "go between" defenders, according to the usual Indian way of designation. Most of the Oglala Sioux warriors were there also. Warriors in warrior society groups from all of the other tribes in the great aggregation of camps were scattered at other points to form a complete encirclement of the soldiers.

Although most of the groupings were by tribes and by warrior societies, with each maintaining its own section of the encirclement, there were many individuals shifting from one place to another. This was a common practice among the Indians so that they could achieve personal coups. Because of this characteristic method of fighting, every Indian narrative of the battle centers mainly upon the individual's personal movements—where he went and what he did or failed to do.

Powder smoke and dust obscured the view of both soldiers and warriors. Since all of them were on foot or lying on the ground or otherwise concealed, the soldiers saw little of the warriors and the warriors saw little of the soldiers. In this regard, however, the warriors had some advantage. Because the soldiers were in the middle, their powder smoke was thick about them. The warriors could thus fire at random into the powder smoke and annoy the soldiers, even if they did no serious physical harm. The same powder smoke hindered the soldiers from seeing clearly out toward the exterior. On the other hand, although the warriors were not hindered by thick smoke about themselves, their separate puffs of smoke were more visible, and individual warriors could be pinpointed when such puffs were seen. For this reason, many Indians shot arrows that curved down into the soldiers' smoke, since the location of the shooter was not revealed.

For about an hour and a half the fighting was slow, with little damage done to the Indians and none, as far as the Indians know, done to the soldiers. All during that time there were, of course, eager individual young warriors striving to creep forward and make coup touches upon soldiers. One such warrior showed the author where he crept forward during the battle and stole a soldier's pack. Frequently, a warrior would mount his pony and race in front of the soldiers as an act of bravado. One Sioux rider was killed during that sort of exhibition. A veteran Cheyenne named Walks Last told the author: "I rode my pony in a fast run past the Custer soldiers. Many of them shot at me. My pony was killed. When it went down, I stayed down by it a short time, and then I crawled away. No bullet touched me."

Although there was a continual creeping forward and frequent exhibitions of bareback pony riding during the hour and a half of slow fighting, it appears that nothing that had any important bearing on the outcome of the battle occurred in that time. It was all very showy but almost harmless, in the usual Indian style.

Then, however, there was a slight change in the soldier tactics, which soon transformed the battle's course. A body of soldiers mounted their horses and dashed from the eastern section of the ridge down toward the river, where the Cheyenne and Oglala Sioux were stationed. The Indians estimate that between 30 and

40 men were involved, and they suppose that the white men were trying to get to the camps. Army officers later identified the bodies as being those of Lieutenant Algernon E. Smith and his troop, and the opinion of army officers is that Custer sent them as a show of aggressiveness that might check and depress the spirits of the Indians. It might be, though, that his prime motive was to cheer up his own men.

The move was an unfortunate one. It inaugurated a series of incidents that followed each other in speedy succession and terminated in a colossal disaster never equaled in the military operations on our American frontier.

At first, the Cheyenne and Oglala shrank back from the charge of the soldiers coming from the ridge. But the charging white men stopped on a low ridge about 500 yards down the gulch slope from the present monument. There they dismounted for a battle stand. A few Cheyenne and Oglala held their ground, remaining hidden in their positions. These unyielding warriors were inspired by Lame White Man.

Lame White Man is a relatively unknown figure in Custer battle writings, but he looms large in the Indian thoughts of that occasion. At times he is referred to by another name, Black Body. In the minds of the Indians, he was the foremost warrior in the battle. A tribal chief of the Southern Cheyenne, he and his wife and two young daughters happened to be sojourning then with the Northern Cheyenne tribe. Little Wolf, the leading chief of the Northern Cheyenne and the principal chief of the Elk warrior society, was not with the tribe that day, so Lame White Man was selected to lead the Elk warriors. He was 37 years old and had been in many battles against white men. Doubtless, he had learned something about how to terrify them. In any case, on this occasion his exhortations and example soon rallied all of the Cheyenne and Oglala warriors. In a few minutes they were all around that small body of soldiers, creeping—and in some cases rushing—forward upon them.

The soldiers' horses began to get excited. The Indian odor always excited horses accustomed only to white men. Conversely, Indian ponies were always frightened by the white man odor. The soldiers' horses became unmanageable. They broke loose from the horseholders and stampeded. In their headlong plunges to get away from the Indians they crashed back and forth among the soldiers before breaking out from the encirclement. The warriors then herded them toward the river. This was an easy task because the day was hot and the horses were thirsty and, in many cases, wounded. They quite naturally went toward water.

Just after the soldiers had dismounted, one of them was seen to jerk his revolver to his head and shoot himself. Soon afterward another, and then another, did the same act. The self-shooting continued when the horses were plunging among them. During that time, and after the horses were gone, it appeared that the soldiers were fighting among themselves. They were shooting each other as well as shooting themselves. Led by Lame White Man, some of the warriors rushed in to make coup strokes upon the enemy or to seize guns from them. According to the Indians, some of the soldiers dropped their rifles and began running wildly here and there so that they were easy victims of the long lance or the tomahawk. Within four or five minutes, according to the estimates of veteran warriors, every one of those soldiers was dead. Moreover, almost all of those deaths were from some cause other than Indian action.

Three warriors were killed while those 30 or 40 soldiers were perishing. One of the dead warriors was an Oglala Sioux. Another was a 17-year-old Cheyenne known as Noisy Walking. The third was Lame White Man. The general turmoil was such that the Indians did not learn that Lame White Man had been killed until after the end of the entire battle. Although almost all of the other warriors were on foot, he led the charge against the soldiers on his pony. The dead pony was found later and its footprints were trailed back. He had gone through the band of soldiers, had traveled some distance beyond them toward the main battle ridge, had turned, and was riding back through the band when he was killed.

Immediately after the incident on the lower slope, a similar thing occurred on the eastern extremity of the main battle ridge. The Sioux warriors around those soldiers got the horses into a stampede. In this instance, too, the horses crashed to and fro among the soldiers before breaking out into a complete escape. Likewise in this instance, the warriors surged forward and the soldiers turned their guns upon themselves. The whirlwind of horses stampeding and soldiers panicking swept westward along the ridge. Within ten minutes, according to the estimates of veteran warriors, no soldiers were left alive except a few at the west end of the ridge, where the monument is now located. The warrior death losses up to that time had been very light, about seven or eight.

That few minutes of quick action after the stampeding of the horses is the period of time recalled by old Indians who refer to the conflict as having lasted "about long enough to smoke a pipeful of tobacco," or "about as long as it takes me to eat breakfast," or some other similar way of estimating time. That culminating tempestuous mix-up was in the mind of the widow of Spotted Horn Bull when she told James McLaughlin, author of *My Friend the Indian* (1910): "It was done very quickly. What was done that day was done while the sun stood still and the white men were delivered into the hands of the Sioux."

The Indian idea of the Custer soldiers destroying themselves is not a later fabrication. It is as old as their first stories of the affair. It could be read between the lines of all of the statements of veteran warriors—when they could be induced to make a statement. If an inquirer felt he already knew much about the matter and simply wanted corroboration of his preconceptions, he usually got that and nothing else. Old Indians are not argumentative, and they ordinarily avoid assertions that might be controverted. Indeed, to learn the straight truth as the old Indian sees it, the following rule must be kept in mind: Wait, wait, wait, don't talk, never contradict, wait again, wait further—simply listen, do nothing but listen.

White interviewers of old Indians have too often been in a hurry. They have had to catch the next train, or something else has impelled them to speed up an interview. But old Indians do not "speed up." Their natural way is to begin at the beginning and go thoughtfully and thoroughly through to the ending. One should not expect that they will tell in a few days or a few hours what they usually impart over the course of weeks, months, or years. Furthermore, their stories are often told in symbolism or are mingled with symbols that have to be understood in order to grasp the full meaning of what they are saying.

One illustration of an interviewer not understanding the story of a veteran Custer battle warrior describing how the soldiers lost the battle is exhibited in a book by Frank B. Linderman published in 1930. It is a good book about Indians, but the author shows that he misunderstood when, in 1887, he hired a veteran warrior to tell of the Custer encounter.

According to the interviewer, the Indian scooped up dust with his hands and formed a mound or ridge to represent the elevation where the Custer soldiers took their stand. He gathered many little sticks, peeled the bark from them, and stuck them upright in array all along the dust heap. These represented the soldiers. After they had been put into position, he shifted some of them, then made other shifts. All of the preparation and the arranging and rearranging were done deliberately. It must have taken an hour or more—about the length of time consumed in the actual fighting at the Custer battle. Then the Indian spit into each of his hands, seized the little sticks, swept them up, threw them away, and brushed his palms over each other. That was the end of the story.

The young man interviewer was disappointed, disgusted. He felt that he had been cheated, that he had not been told anything. The Indian had quit just when it seemed he was ready to begin. In fact, the narrator had faithfully fulfilled his promise. He had depicted the essential features of the event from beginning to end. His actions and gestures were symbols intended to convey exactly what happened. He told that the soldiers were on an elevation of land. They changed positions there from time to time. This lasted for an hour or more—the length of time was symbolized by the time the Indian consumed in his deliberate proceedings, which were mistaken by the interviewer as indicative of dullness in thought. The sudden and violent discarding of the little sticks meant that the soldiers "threw themselves away," an expression often used by the veteran warriors in both their sign language and their verbal accounts of what the Custer soldiers did. The spitting into the hands—in fact, it regularly is done against the fingers—meant that the soldiers shot each other or fought among themselves. The brushing of the palms over each other is usually put into words as "all gone." But when this gesture is used in reference to the Custer soldiers, it is commonly translated into words as "wiped out." It seems, though, that the best interpretation in the Custer battle case is "they vanished from existence."

There are variations in the old Indian explanations as to precisely how the Custer soldier self-destruction occurred. In fact, the Indians are somewhat bewildered about the matter. They actually saw only a few suicides and only a few incidences of one soldier shooting another soldier. Clear views were hindered by the fact that all of the white men and all of the Indian warriors were lying on the ground or were creeping or were otherwise moving carefully here and there on the field. The definite statements of the veteran Indians have been mainly that there was much shooting going on among the soldiers themselves, and that afterward it was discovered that all of them were dead. They generally agree that the Almighty, in some way or other, caused the white men to die in penalty for having come to kill unoffending Indians.

One theory is that a clap of thunder or a flash of lightning, perceptible only to the medicine men, did the entire work in an instant. Another theory is that the soldiers were caused to go insane and to mistake each other for enemies who should be killed. Still another variation is that the prayers of the medicine men created around the soldiers an encirclement of a transparent barrier, which resembled glass but was impenetrable by bullets. When the soldiers shot their guns at the Indians, the bullets rebounded and killed the soldiers. This fantasy symbolizes the idea that, in all phases of life, every wrongful act toward a fellow being will recoil and inflict harm upon the one who initiates it.

Suicide to avoid capture in warfare was not known among Indians themselves. Therefore, it was beyond their thought patterns to conceive of white men committing such an act voluntarily with premeditation. There undoubtedly had been many previous instances of white men committing suicide to avoid capture by Indians, and the Indians probably had observed many such instances. But their mental make-up and their warrior ways led them naturally to infer that suicides in time of battle always were involuntary, caused by insanity or by extraneous compulsion. Moreover, no Indian could see why any Custer soldier would kill himself, since the Indians had no thought of trying to capture them alive.

Soldier drunkenness became the standard explanation given by Indians to casual inquirers. It appears that this really was the belief of a few of the Indians at the time of the battle. But it did not have the deep roots and the wide prevalence of the beliefs in miraculous intervention. As time passed on, the explanations involving mystic action were ridiculed by white men and by Indians who were educated in schools. On the other hand, the explanation that the soldiers were drunk was more acceptable to the inquiring whites and the school-educated Indians. Thus, the old Indians—influenced partly by a wish to avoid ridicule or controversy and partly by thoughts that maybe the inquirers had superior knowledge enabling them to know the real truth— acceded to the drunkenness explanation. The genuine old Indian conception of the event can only be learned by waiting and listening as the story gradually unfolds. Even if some one or another old Indian actually accepts the drunkenness theory as true, it may be assumed that down deep he harbors a firm belief that the Everywhere Spirit saw to it that the whiskey was provided for that purpose.

A Cheyenne old woman was the first narrator who plainly told the author of the soldiers' suicides. While she was speaking, two veteran warriors who had been at the battle and one man who had been a youth, but not a warrior, at that time were present. None of these men indicated either assent or dissent as the old woman related what the soldiers had done—or what the Almighty had done to them. A few days later the man who had been a youth at the time of the battle repeated the old woman's story and added some details of his own. One of the veteran warriors then followed up with his corroborations of what had been said. Thus was opened the vein wherein appears to have been discovered the key to the mystery of Custer's last battle.

The course of those interviews could have been quite different under other conditions. If there had been a manifestation of disbelief of the old woman, the man who had been a youth at the battle would not have told his story. Instead, he would have joined in a general discrediting of her as being merely a woman and, therefore, one who knew nothing about such matters. If any incredulity had been shown when the younger man told his story, both this nonwarrior and the old woman would have been disparaged by the veteran warriors as foolish and irresponsible. So the matter would have been kept unrevealed, and the author would have gathered only inconsequential or well-known generalities about a sturdy struggle to the end.

Demented people were regarded by old-time Indians with awe. This feeling applies to the case of the Custer soldiers, because they were demented according to the Indian idea of their case. For this reason, the veteran warriors are usually reluctant to talk about them other than in obscure or indirect terms. Also, many of the veteran warriors have been reluctant to visit the scene where so powerful an exhibition of mystic influences occurred. One of the veteran warriors who accompanied the author to the battlefield exhibited this ingrained reverence. Hour after hour, through two successive long summer days in 1928, he pointed out precise spots and told what had happened at those spots. But at every large group of the marble slabs marking the positions of dead bodies on the battlefield he balked and remained 30 to 40 feet away. He did his recalling and narrating from a distance, refusing to go in among any of the slab groups. His explanation— which was accepted without question or comment—was that "if I go there I must hide my face."

A comparatively small number of the Custer soldiers were actually seen in suicidal acts. During most of the time of fighting, they were lying on the ground and doing the best they could to keep themselves sheltered from enemy view, and the Indian warriors were doing the same. The hundreds of old men, youths, and boys on their ponies were located on the background hills out of bullet range and were in better position to see. None of them, however, could see all of the white men at all times. The individual testimonies to the author have been of one, two, three, or more self-killings. Tall Bull, a Cheyenne warrior, often recounted that he had seen one soldier shoot and kill three of his companions, one after another, in quick succession. But, for the most part, the Indians merely observed much gunfire going on among the soldiers themselves with no bullets coming toward the Indians, and later they discovered that all of the white men were dead.

Writers have quoted many veteran warriors who found little or no reason to boast about the Custer battle. They had not performed any brave deeds according to their war code. The reason for such belittling of the affair by warriors is that, as far as the Indians are concerned, it was as if the earth suddenly had opened a chasm and swallowed the soldiers. Some of the Indians—the Cheyenne, in particular—later began to include the anniversary date of the Custer battle in their annual tribal religious ceremonies. This has been done, however, not in a spirit of jubilation, but in reverential recognition of the fact that the Everywhere Spirit intervened in that event on behalf of the Indians.

Another factor that has deterred old Indians from speaking openly about the Custer battle is their fancy that white people, who have books and other sources of information not accessible to Indians, know all about every feature of the whole affair. So, the old red people regard it as impolite—or very imprudent— for them to disclose that they saw any conduct unbecoming to brave and good soldiers. Even if a white person would bring up that feature of the battle as a subject for discussion, the Indian would be most hesitant to talk. Such conversation would be possible only after a long period of close and trusted acquaintance. Otherwise, the naturally suspicious Indian would be afraid that he was being led into a trap which might result in verbal or even physical abuse. Undoubtedly, on many occasions flashes of anger or ridicule from white people have caused narrating warriors to retreat from statements or intimations that the Custer soldiers did not fight as well as they might have. Further, all Indian references to those suicides necessitate coupling such actions with their theories of mystic interference as the cause of the acts. Such mystic interference is, of course, discredited by the whites, who are not tolerant of such theories. Thus, an opportunity to learn something new and important has been unwittingly lost.

It is easy to get a misconception of what old Indians tell, even when a good interpreter is present. For example, many times during the author's earlier associations with veteran warriors, one or another of them spoke of seeing Custer, or chasing Custer, or jerking Custer from his horse, or killing Custer, or some such thing. There seemed to be too many people who had personal contact with the leader of the soldiers. It took a long time to discover what the Indians really meant. But finally it became clear that they were using the name Custer as a generic term to designate all the soldiers they encountered on that day, even the members of the Reno and Benteen forces. Rehearings of their stories ultimately revealed that not any one of them really intended to convey the idea that General George A. Custer himself was the soldier especially encountered. It would appear that this generic use of the name Custer has misled a good number of interviewers. As a result, General Custer has been represented as having died on various parts of the battlefield, in the midst of the Little Bighorn River, and even in the Indian camps.

Another misconception has arisen, apparently, from a common warrior statement that "Custer" charged toward the river, that the Indians at first ran away from the charge, and that they then turned and made a successful fight. The author was misled for a time by this feature of their stories. But it became clear that "Custer" referred to the 30 or 40 men who dashed down from the main battle ridge. Many of the men from the Reno and Gibbon forces who inspected the battlefield two days later saw tracks of army horses and a few dead army horses near the river ford, so they concluded that the Custer detachment went there first and then retreated to the battle ridge. It seems evident, though, that these dead horses had been wounded earlier and died at the river when they tried to get a drink of water. The tracks of shod horses were made by the stampeded animals. The Indians stayed in the vicinity all the remainder of that day and until mid-afternoon of the next day. The military examination of the Custer battlefield and its surroundings was made two and three days after the battle. Since the Indians had captured many of the soldiers' horses and had done some riding of them, the investigators could have found tracks all around the battlefield and in the Indian camps. There seems to be no ground for disputing the statements of warriors that no Custer soldier ever got nearer to the river than he was when he died.

The various representations that depict a horde of warriors on horseback charging the Custer soldiers may have arisen from narratives of veteran warriors. But those narratives were misunderstood. As a matter of fact, all of the warriors were on foot, except for an occasional leader or an occasional individual who rode his pony in a daring run past the soldiers. Many hundreds of boys and youths, along with many old men, were on the surrounding ridges and hills, out of bullet range, watching the progress of the battle. They were all on their ponies. When word was circulated that all of the soldiers were dead, those noncombatant horsemen rushed upon the field to make coup strokes upon the dead. That was the final "horseback charge" upon the Custer soldiers. The great "war whoop" that has been associated with their charge was their joining in the tremendous chorus of death-wails.

The small number of Indian deaths at the Custer battle indicates that the soldiers did not resist. Visitors at the battlefield often venture conjectures that hundreds of Indians must have been killed there. This is a natural supposition and it is commonly prevalent. Published writings usually have omitted reference to this matter. In his book, Colonel Graham quotes an estimate of 40 Indians killed and gives his own opinion that the Indian loss was "negligible." Horny Horse, a Hunkpapa Sioux, is quoted in McLaughlin's book as putting the number of dead Indians at between 50 and 60 in the Custer and Reno battles combined. That same book quotes Spotted Horn Bull's widow, whose story is published in full, as specifying the number at 22. Rain-in-the-Face, another Hunkpapa Sioux, told W. Kent Thomas that the number of dead Indians was "ten-and-four or ten-and-six"—meaning 14 or 16. Crow King, still another Hunkpapa, reported to Judson Elliott Walker that there were more than 30 but not as many as 50. Colonel J. W. Pope and Captain W. P. Clark were informed by their Sioux scouts in 1877 that the Indian death loss in all of the Little Bighorn fighting was between 30 and 40. General Sherman's report to the Secretary of War states that it "is variously estimated from 40 to 100."

An estimate of 31, based upon recountings of various veteran warriors, has been settled upon by the author. This is the total of all Indians killed by both the Custer and the Reno forces. Colonel Poland is reported to have learned from his Sioux scouts in 1877 that only a few warriors were killed by the Custer men, and that the major part of the Indian loss was in the fighting against Reno on the hilltop. Veteran warrior informants of the author have generally agreed with that opinion, although a few have said simply that the number of losses was about the same in each case. Striking an average of all veteran warrior opinions on this point, it may be estimated that in the Custer fighting 14 Indians were killed, while in the Reno fighting 17 Indians were killed.

These estimates of warrior losses are consistent with the traditional Indian ideas as to what constituted a loss justifying withdrawal from further battle. It was pointed out earlier that when Indian warriors were attacking from the outside and could leave the field whenever they might choose to do so, they regularly quit because of death losses which they regarded as discouraging, but which by our war customs would be regarded as scant. Often, in discussing the warrior deaths at the Little Bighorn, the author has heard old Indians bewail the loss of 31 of their many hundreds of warriors as having been a great calamity to their people. Chief Little Wolf of the Cheyenne, who arrived at the camps an hour or so after the Custer battle had ended, was surrounded and heckled mercilessly by a mob of both Sioux and Cheyenne for having been absent from the battle. The abuse heaped upon him was on the ground that if he had been there he would have restrained the warriors from taking risks, and so the number of Indian deaths would not have been so great.

White soldiers who saw dead Indian bodies two days after the Custer battle have discussed the matter with the author. One of those informants was Henry G. Rice, who was among Lieutenant Bradley's 12 mounted infantrymen with General Gibbon in 1876. These soldiers arrived at the battle scene on the morning of June 27, 1876, two days after it had occurred. Bradley and his men, including Rice, were the first to discover the dead bodies of Custer and his soldiers. Regarding the Indians killed, Rice said: "I think there were not very many of them. I saw 15 dead warriors in tipis, and there were some more on scaffolds, and two or three in trees. I did not see any dead Indian ponies anywhere there."

Another reliable informant was William H. White, who was with the Second Cavalry arriving with Gibbon. Private White was one of the soldiers assigned to gather tipi poles, buffalo robes, and other materials needed to make litters for carrying Reno's wounded men. To get the necessary items, they tore down the tipis where the dead warriors were lying. White stated:

There were two tipis containing dead Indian bodies. We tore down both of them, to use the material. In one there were five bodies, and in the other there were three. Besides these, there were seven dead bodies on scaffolds. Maybe there were some in trees, but I did not notice any. I did not see any dead Indian ponies anywhere except two lying by burial scaffolds. I suppose they were killed there by the Indians themselves as a part of their burial customs.

Various veteran soldiers have told of a certain incident that occurred between Gibbon and Reno after the arrival of Gibbon and his soldiers at Reno's hill position on the morning of June 27. Gibbon twitted Reno in this way: "I have seen many dead soldiers and dead soldier horses in this vicinity, but I have not seen many dead Indians nor dead ponies." This sort of twitting is said to have been repeated until General Terry suggested that some other topic of conversation would be better.

One might think that a large number of dead warriors were carried away when the Indians left the scene. But the Indians would only transfer their dead as far as was necessary to find a suitable place of burial. It was quite common for Sioux burials to be made simply by abandoning a home tipi—often with all of its contents included—which then served as a shelter for the dead who were left lying on the ground or on a scaffold built inside the tipi. The usual Cheyenne custom was to make burials in mountain caves or on top of the ground on hilltops. The body was wrapped in a buffalo robe and then covered with stones.

One might also think that the Indians were in a hurry to get away and were thus unable to take all of their dead with them, so that the dead warriors found by the Gibbon soldiers were simply the remaining few of an original large number. The idea that the Indians did hurry in going away has been regarded as supported by the fact that some tipis were found standing with all of the household property in them, and that many utensils and other personal belongings were left at the campsites. But it was customary among all of the Plains Indians for a mourning family either to abandon or to tear down and destroy any tipi in which a relative had died. Further, the mourning survivors either gave away or threw away all of their belongings and put themselves into destitution. The 31 deaths caused 31 tipis to be abandoned or otherwise discarded and caused the contents of all of those tipis to be thrown away.

That wreckage was what the Gibbon soldiers found two days

after the battle. It was deduced that the Indians departed in such a hurry that they left behind much property as well as their dead. But, considering the Indians' mourning customs, it is evident that the quantity of abandoned property was proportionate to the number of dead. If more property had been found, it would have meant that more warriors had been killed.

The warriors began quitting the Reno Hill battle just after noon on Monday, June 26, and by the middle of the afternoon practically all of them had gone back to the camps. Soon afterward, the Reno men saw the long procession of all the tribes going south up the Little Bighorn Valley. At that time, the Gibbon soldiers were several miles down the valley. About sunset the soldiers set up their camp more than a mile from the extreme edges of where the Indian encampments had been. They saw warriors on the hills, but the Gibbon people did not learn until the next morning that there had been a great Indian encampment and a great battle.

The old Indians have persisted in denying that they left the scene because of fear of the Gibbon soldiers. They usually have said that their reason for going was that they had lost too many warriors. Several Indians, including Sitting Bull, have added that the soldier loss had been all that it needed to be. In fact, almost half of the Seventh Cavalry regiment had been killed. It is not unlikely that the Indians' warfare rule of relenting in battle if half of the opponents were killed was applied in that instance. Moreover, it is not unlikely that the same rule might have been applied in the segregate instance of the Custer detachment if that fighting had been continued as genuine fighting until half of the soldiers were killed by the Indians.

It may be noted that the number of dead warriors seen by White and Rice, the two Gibbon soldiers quoted, is somewhat lower than the number that the author has settled upon as the Indian loss. In explanation it should be considered that the Cheyenne, obedient to their custom, took their six dead warriors for interment in neighboring hillside caves. These were not found by the Gibbon soldiers nor by any other white observers, so far as is publicly known. This would leave 25 dead warriors somewhere about the campsites. But, although the Sioux usually buried their dead on an outdoor scaffold or on the ground of a tipi shelter, they occasionally placed them in caves or in trees. Some bodies may have been in the trees beside the Little Bighorn River, hidden by the full foliage of late June.

It is interesting to compare the estimated 14 warriors killed by the 213 Custer men with some credible estimates of the number of warriors killed by the 81 Fetterman-Brown men during the 21 minutes they mingled with Indian warriors in 1866. Red Cloud, the leading Oglala Sioux chief at the time of that brief encounter, informed his old white friend, Captain James Cook, of Agate, Nebraska, that 11 warriors were killed by those soldiers. Two Moons, a Cheyenne warrior chief, said that the warrior dead at that battle numbered 14—1 Arapaho, 2 Cheyenne, and 11 Sioux. Discussing the Fetterman Fight in his book, Custer says that the Indians "acknowledged afterwards to have suffered a loss of 12 killed on the field."

All of the stories of the veteran warriors disclose a panic of the Custer soldiers. Their narratives indicating it are supported by the fact that their own death loss in the conflict was about 14. A consideration of both the Indian customs for disposing of their dead and the observations of the Gibbon soldiers corroborate the Indian death loss figures, and these figures tend to confirm the Indian stories about the conduct of the soldiers.

THE DREAD OF TORTURE

The customary Indian treatment of enemies surrendering themselves has been discussed earlier. It was pointed out that their normally chivalric warfare code may not have been applied in dealing with whites because, from the Indian point of view, the whites did not fight in an honorable manner. It may have been, then, that white captives were treated more cruelly than Indian captives. Certainly, whites believed that there was no race of people who could be more brutally cruel than the Indians when they felt in the mood. It seems, however, that deliberate and methodical torturing of captives was much less common among Indian tribes than has been represented. It seems further that it was extremely uncommon for them to make special effort to capture an enemy for the particular purpose of torturing him.

No matter what the real character of the Indians was, however, their reputed character created in the minds of all whites an agonizing dread of being captured by them in warfare. That terror in the minds of whites fighting against them existed throughout our frontier history, including the period surrounding 1876. A sampling of published expressions from the Plains frontier era may exemplify the feelings common to all white people—soldiers as well as civilians—about the Indians' torturing of captives.

Writing in *Frontier Dust*, John Lord tells of himself and Dick Hook having been pursued by Indians on the Platte River in the early 1870s. They made a mutual agreement: "If I am wounded so I can't ride, don't leave me alive, and I will do the same for you." A veteran soldier in Texas, telling about his experiences in a magazine, in 1932, included this: "When we fought with the Indians we had to fight for our lives, because they took no prisoners, or, if they did, only to torture them to death." A veteran of the Eleventh Kansas Cavalry, writing about the Platte Bridge Fight, which occurred in 1865, dwells upon supposed tortures of wounded soldiers left on the field there. Speaking of one body that could not be found, the writer says: "It may have been possible that the Indians captured him and carried him away to torture at one of their villages."

In 1863 there was an expedition of 15 miners from Bannack City, Montana Territory, to the Yellowstone River and into the Bighorn Mountains. Samuel T. Hauser, who afterward became governor of Montana Territory, was one of those miners. Governor Hauser's account of their experiences was published in the Montana Historical Society collections. According to him, Indians threatened them from time to time. Finally, they made an attack upon the miners' camp. The fighting continued through some hours. During that time a suicidal pact was made by the white men. Hauser says:

> Geery, Underwood, and myself, who belonged to the "fraternity," had a little side talk which resulted in each one declaring that if he got wounded he would reserve one shot that should prevent unnecessary sacrifice of the party by remaining to defend a man that must soon die anyway, and also to prevent torture if captured. I talked it over with Jim, and finally with all the rest, who all came to the same agreement.

Two of those men were seriously wounded. Immediately after the Indians withdrew from the fight, one of the wounded men committed suicide. While the miners were packing up to go, the other wounded man put his revolver to his head and sent a fatal bullet into his own head.

That soldiers thought along this same vein is revealed in the story of S. S. Peters, a veteran who had been with General Carrington in 1866. At that time, Carrington was establishing Forts Reno, Phil Kearny, and C. F. Smith on the Bozeman Trail in Wyoming and Montana. Peters was with a body of soldiers going from Fort Reno toward the proposed new Fort Phil Kearny. Oglala Sioux Indians attacked them on July 20, 1866.

All of the officers and men in this soldier body were seasoned veterans of the Civil War, according to Peters' story. The officers included Lieutenants A. H. Wands, James H. Bradley, P. M. Skinner, George H. Templeton, and Napoleon H. Daniels. Two civilians and two women—wives of officers—were with them. The military people made a corral of their wagons and barricaded themselves for a defensive fight. The assault of the Indians lasted two or three hours. Lieutenant Daniels and Sergeant Terrel were killed. The Indians finally left the scene. Nevertheless, while the battle was in progress the white men determined upon the following course: "It was solemnly decided that in case it came to the worst we would mercifully kill all the wounded and the two women and then ourselves."

On December 20, 1866, Captains Fetterman and Brown, with soldiers and a few civilians accompanying them, were killed to the last man in what is often known as the Fetterman Massacre. It was commonly said that the men in the Fetterman-Brown forces were "slowly tortured to death." It was also commonly accepted without dispute that both Captain Fetterman and Captain Brown committed suicide, or that they killed each other in consummation of a suicidal pact, in that battle. According to one version: "Seeing that all was lost, they had evidently stood face to face, and each had shot the other dead with his revolver." The military never denied this supposed action of the two officers. It appears to have been considered that their course was a natural one, merely a great misfortune.

What is known as the Wagon Box Fight took place near Fort Phil Kearny on August 2, 1867, seven and a half months after the Fetterman Fight. In the book *The Bozeman Trail* (1922), Sergeant Samuel Gibson relates his experiences in the Wagon Box Fight. When the soldiers saw the Indians coming, they prepared to hold a position in the wagon boxes which had been put into defensive array. Gibson tells of a notable preparation that was taken by some of his companions—and, probably, by himself too. The men connected shoestrings together to form a long cord with a small loop at each end. One loop was for hooking over the big toe and the other was for hooking on the trigger of a rifle. That preparation was for a last-resort act. As Gibson expresses it, they would take that action "rather than be captured and made to endure the inevitable torture." Among those taking the grim precautionary measure was Sergeant Frank Robertson, the oldest veteran among them. Gibson says that he knew that "the red devils would never get old Frank Robertson alive."

R. J. Smith, who was in the Wagon Box Fight, wrote his story for Cyrus Townsend Brady's *Indian Fights and Fighters* (1923). He says that at all times during the fight he was reserving two cartridges for himself, "in case of a showdown." A story by F. G. Burnett appears in *The Bozeman Trail*. Burnett was a participant in what is known as the Hayfield Fight, near Fort C. F. Smith on August 1, 1867. He tells of one soldier there who had to be restrained from committing suicide because of fear that the Indians would get him and torture him.

In 1876 that same idea of suicide "in case of a showdown" was still prevalent—and, perhaps, even more strongly fixed in soldier minds. Some army officers who were in the 1876 campaign and who later wrote of its events included in their writings a reference to the certainty of torture if any soldier had been captured alive that year. They also referred to the probable torture of a few who apparently were captured during that time. Generals Charles King and Guy V. Henry, who were minor officers with Crook in 1876, wrote fervently of the matter. General Godfrey, a lieutenant with the Seventh Cavalry in 1876, touched upon the subject. Captain John G. Bourke, who was with Crook in 1876, recorded his feelings in his narrative of the destruction of the Cheyenne camp on March 17. He states that three soldiers were killed, one was mortally wounded, and six others received wounds in varying degrees. It appears that one of those wounded soldiers was left on the field when the main body of troops departed from the scene. Bourke writes of the horror expressed in the subsequent conversations of the soldiers about the fate of the abandoned comrade.

John F. Finerty, a newspaper man, was with Crook during all of that summer of campaigning. He later wrote *War-Path and Bivouac* (1890). In the preface of the book he discusses in general the dangers risked by soldiers in those times. His description culminates in the following statement: "Our soldiers who were disabled in the Indian campaigns had ever before them the terrors of fiendish torture and mutilation in case of capture by the savages."

After the Rosebud battle on June 17, 1876, and during July, Crook had his little army encamped at the mouth of Goose Creek, near the present Sheridan, Wyoming. On July 7, Lieutenant Frederick W. Sibley was sent out from camp with a band of soldiers to scout the neighboring country to learn if any Indians were around. Finerty went with the Sibley scouting party. They found Indians—or, rather, the Indians, a band of Cheyenne warriors, found the soldiers. The Cheyenne attacked, and an hour or so of skirmish fighting ensued, with the soldiers on the retreat.

According to Finerty, Lieutenant Sibley admonished his soldiers: "If retreat should prove impossible let no man surrender. Die in your tracks, because Indians show no mercy." Finerty goes on to describe the course of the battle:

> As the volume of the Indian fire seemed to increase, "No surrender" was the word passed around the thin skirmish line. Each of us would, if he found it necessary, have blown out his own brains rather than fall alive into Indian hands.

Elizabeth Custer's books reveal something of the customary thoughts and talk in the Seventh Cavalry, from the time of its first 1867 campaign, regarding suicide as a means to avoid capture by the Indians. In *Tenting on the Plains* (1888), she writes about an incident in which that type of action was regarded as applicable. The incident occurred as the Seventh Cavalry was returning to Fort Wallace from their campaign north of that post in the summer of 1867. Their wagon train was attacked by Cheyenne Indians near Fort Wallace. It had been planned that Mrs. Custer should go by ambulance from Fort Riley to Fort Wallace and meet her husband when he returned there. The ambulance was to accompany the wagon train. But, just as she was about to leave, the commanding officer at Fort Riley ordered her not to go. When the fight against the wagon train was about to begin, Lieutenant William Cooke, who was with troops hurrying to assist the wagon guard, hurried first to learn if Mrs. Custer was in the ambulance. She was not, so he returned to the soldiers. Discussing the case afterwards, Cooke told her that if she had been in the ambulance he would have shot her to death before giving any orders to the soldiers.

In *Boots and Saddles* (1885), Mrs. Custer writes that it was generally understood in the regiment that, if it became probable that she would be captured by Indians, she was to be shot dead by whoever might have her in charge at the time. In the same book she writes of a time when Indians threatened Fort Abraham Lincoln, and the main body of the regiment went out to resist them. During the absence of their men, the women talked seriously among themselves about the matter of committing suicide or killing each other if the Indians got into the fort.

Military records show that General Carrington, on an occasion at Fort Phil Kearny, contemplated that a wholesale killing of women and children at the post might be necessary. The occasion was the day after the Fetterman-Brown soldiers were overwhelmed by the encircling tornado of Oglala Sioux and Cheyenne. Carrington was about to go with his remaining soldiers, except for a few guards, to retrieve the bodies of the men killed the day before. He left with the guard officer a written order, which included this statement:

> If, in my absence, Indians in overwhelming numbers attack, put the women and children in the magazine, with supplies of water, bread and crackers, and other supplies that seem best, and, in the event of a last desperate struggle, destroy all together, rather than have any captured alive.

In Carrington's subsequent official report of the battle in which Fetterman, Brown, and 79 others had been killed he stated this opinion: "As Brown always declared he would reserve a shot for himself as a last resort, I am convinced that he and Fetterman fell by each other's hand rather than undergo the slow torture inflicted upon others."

General Custer's book reveals that he gave thought to the matter of suicide as a last resort. When speaking of the campaign in 1867, he discussed in general the horrors of Indian torture. Before that, after reviewing the case of the Fetterman Fight, Custer says: "Colonel Fetterman and Captain Brown no doubt inflicted this death upon themselves. These officers had often asserted that they would never be taken alive by Indians."

The subject of suicide came pointedly to Custer's notice on one occasion in the spring of 1869, on the southern Plains. He was about to start with a small detachment of his men on a search for a camp of hostile Apache Indians. Just as Custer had mounted his horse and was about to set out, a junior officer who was remaining in the camp came forward and slipped a loaded derringer pistol into the General's hand. The action was accompanied by a quiet and serious admonition: "You had better take it, General. It may prove useful to you."

The book contains no clear statement as to whether Custer accepted or rejected the offered pistol, or whether he approved or disapproved of the significance of the offer. A tacit approval of it is intimated insofar as he does not mention having reprimanded the subordinate or having considered himself as offended in the least. It appears to have been regarded simply as an act that

showed earnest interest in his welfare and was not at all unbecoming.

Such tacit approval of last-resort suicide runs through all of the
writings founded on Plains Indian warfare. All the writings of
both officers and enlisted men treat it as an accepted course of
action. Plains frontiersmen make similar references to Indian torture and to suicide as the sole mode of escape from it. In fact,
the frontiersmen taught it to the soldiers and other latecomers.

This idea was not restricted to our western Plains or even to
our part of the world. It has probably been harbored in all parts
of the world wherever soldiers of established governments have
encountered wild tribes. British troops in Asia were not unmindful
of it. Rudyard Kipling noted it in poetic lines:

> When you're wounded and left on Afghanistan's plains,
> And the women come out to cut up what remains,
> Jest roll to your rifle and blow out your brains
> And go to your Gawd like a soldier.

There is evidence that forebodings of tragedy were in the minds
of some of the Seventh Cavalry when they were on the Indians'
trail. Thoughts of suicide may have prompted the gambler who
deposited his money with Godfrey. At another place in his writings, Godfrey tells of events at the mouth of the Rosebud:

> As soon as it was determined that we were to go out,
> nearly every one took time to write letters home, but I doubt
> very much if there were many of a cheerful nature. Some of
> the officers made their wills. Others gave verbal instructions
> as to the disposition of personal property and distribution
> of mementoes. They seemed to have a presentiment of their
> fate.

Godfrey says that on the night of June 26, when the remaining
men of the Seventh Cavalry were on the hilltop, there was talk
among them of the probability that some of their lost comrades
were then undergoing torture in the Indian camps.

Some of the Reno men later testified that during the time of
the fighting they gave intensive thought to suicide as an alternative to torture. Private Thomas O'Neil, who was left behind with
Lieutenant DeRudio when the Reno men fled from their timber
position, was one who expressed himself in this matter. In his
story, which is included in the Brininstool book, he wrote: "There
was no use surrendering, as it only meant death by the most horrible form of torture." Theodore Golden, in his testimony at the
Reno trial, spoke of another instance. Referring to the wounded

soldier being treated by Dr. Porter when they left the timber position, Golden testified that the man implored: "Don't leave me here to be tortured by these fiends."

Private Peter Thompson was another who wrote of the suicide alternative. He was in the Custer detachment moving toward the Indian camps. According to his published story, his horse became exhausted, so he had to remain behind and hide along the gulches and in the timber by the river. That night of June 25 he joined the Reno forces on the hilltop. At various times during the afternoon, it seemed that the Indians were going to discover him. On each occasion he prepared to resist them. He wrote: "I made up my mind that all but one shot would be fired at the Indians, and that one would go into my own head, for I had determined never to be taken alive."

Suicide was something deeply engraved in the mind of every soldier engaged in Indian warfare in those times. Undoubtedly, when the warriors encircled Custer's men, and as the encirclement drew closer and the horses were stampeded, every white man there, including the commanding officer, recalled the old-time rule of the Plains: "When fighting Indians, keep the last bullet for yourself."

BULLETS GONE CRAZY

The first scant news of the Custer battle came to Generals Terry and Gibbon and their followers at the mouth of the Little Bighorn River on the morning of Monday, June 26, 1876, the day after the event. Some Crow Indian scouts who had escaped from the battle scene stood at a distance from a detachment of the Terry-Gibbon forces and gave a sketchy message in sign language that all of the Custer soldiers had been killed. Then the scouts hastened on toward their home agency. The information they gave was thought to mean only that there had been an encounter with the hostile Indians. The report of annihilation was rejected as being beyond the bounds of possibility, as being simply an exaggeration of Indian fancy. But 24 hours later it was learned that the Indian scouts' report was true.

Major Reno and his men on the hilltop knew nothing of the gory affair until the Terry-Gibbon forces arrived on Tuesday morning, and Lieutenant Bradley and his 12 mounted infantrymen brought the astounding report of what they had discovered on the battle ridge. The soldiers were amazed. In this regard, all of their subsequent recountings and all of the testimony at the Reno trial may be suitably represented by Lieutenant Varnum's statement: "The idea of Custer's command having been all killed never entered my mind."

The report of the Indian scouts was not an exaggeration of fancy. This was proved with shocking certainty. But, what about the stories of veteran warriors concerning panic and self-destruction among the Custer soldiers? Were these exaggerations of Indian fancy? It seems fitting now to examine some of the pertinent statements and opinions of army officers of that time.

General Philip Sheridan's report, dated November 25, 1876, contains this comment:

> Custer, with his tired men and horses, became, I am afraid, an easy prey to the enemy. Their wild savage yells, overwhelming numbers, and frightening war paraphernalia made it as much as any trooper could do to take care of his horse, thus endangering his own safety and efficiency.

Lieutenant Colonel Mike Sheridan examined the battlefield one year after the battle. He testified at the Reno trial in 1879. He said he found indications that the men in Lieutenant James Calhoun's troop had been fighting in normal skirmish line, and he added: "There was no other place where there was evidence of resistance." Further on in his testimony he repeated: "From the position of the bodies of Captain Calhoun's company it looked to me as though that was the only point where resistance was made at all."

The officers in the Reno and Benteen forces explored the Custer field on the third and fourth days after the battle. Some of them gave testimony at the Reno trial about the conditions they observed at the time they were there. The officers who clearly expressed themselves in this regard were Captains Benteen and Moylan, and Lieutenants DeRudio, Hare, and Wallace.

Lieutenant Hare, recalling his observations among the bodies at the eastern part of the ridge and on the lower slope, testified: "I saw no cartridge shells of ours at all."

Lieutenant DeRudio, discussing the conditions over the field in general, said: "I saw only a few cartridge shells."

Captain Moylan, speaking of conditions in the Calhoun group, said he counted 28 shells around one man. He said further: "There was no evidence of organized or sustained resistance on Custer field except around Calhoun."

Lieutenant Wallace testified: "They were not killed in order, but were scattered irregularly all over. At one or two places I saw little piles of shells, 25 or 30. This was near where Calhoun was killed. Very few elsewhere."

Captain Benteen covered the subject more extensively than any of the other officers. Several excerpts from his testimony follow:

> There was no line on the battlefield. You can take a hand-
> ful of corn and scatter it over the floor and make just such
> lines—none at all. The only approach to a line was where five
> or six horses were found at equal distances like skirmishers.
> Ahead of them were five or six men at about the same dis-
> tances, showing that the horses were killed and that the
> riders jumped off and were all heading to get where General
> Custer was.
>
> The position of the bodies on Custer battlefield indicated
> that the officers did not die with their companies. That shows
> that they did not fight by companies. All of the officers except
> Colonel Keogh, Captain Calhoun, and Lieutenant Crittenden
> were on the line with Custer. That would not be a fact if the
> command were overwhelmed while making a stand.
>
> I went over the battlefield carefully, with a view to deter-
> mining how the battle was fought. I arrived at the conclusion
> as I have now—that it was a rout, a panic, till the last man
> was killed.
>
> Many orders might have been given, but few obeyed. I
> think they were panic-stricken. It was a rout, as I said before.

Benteen differed slightly from the officers who attributed resistance to the Calhoun troop, but he agreed with the veteran
warriors when he said: "Only where General Custer was found
was there evidence of a stand." Another significant statement in
Benteen's testimony is: "I counted 70 dead horses and 2 Indian
ponies." Some officers spoke of seeing only one dead pony; others
did not see any.

It is thus clear that the representations of a mass charge by a
horde of warriors on horseback are far from true. If such a charge
had taken place, with soldiers shooting constantly at the advanc-
ing warriors, as is shown in some paintings of the battle, there
would have been scores or hundreds of dead ponies on the field.
Instead, one or two dead ponies were found there. That image of
a horseback charge is usually coupled with a picture of hundreds
of dead warriors. The presence of so few dead warriors in the
vicinity of the vacated campsites is explained away with the
misconceived statement that the Indians always carried away
their dead. But, did the Indians carry away all but two of their
dead ponies?

The standard cavalry method, in any case of dismounting to
fight a pitched battle, was to tie the horses together, bit-to-bit,
in groups of four. One horseholder was assigned to each group

of four horses. So, for the Custer detachment, which totaled 213 men, about 54 of them would have been holding the horses. It is probable that the Indians made special efforts to harass or to kill those guardians and thus to release the horses for the Indians to capture and keep. It is not likely that the Indians intentionally shot any horse, since capture of those animals had an important place in their concept of warfare. It may be presumed, then, that all, or almost all, of the 70 dead horses counted by Captain Benteen were shot by the soldiers so they would not get away with the ammunition or so their bodies could be used as barricades. Observers agree that the largest number of dead horses were found at the west end of the battle ridge, where Custer's body was discovered together with the largest group of dead soldiers.

The number of horses stampeded by the Indians may be computed by deducting the 70 dead from the original 213. Captain Keogh's horse, which was badly wounded, was found two or three days later by the Reno men and was nursed back to health. It appears, then, that the Indians got away with 142 of the soldiers' horses. It may be that not all of them were being held bit-to-bit in groups of four. Or, it may be that some of them jerked themselves loose or tore off their bridles in their rampant terror. No discussion of this point by the officers has come to the notice of the author, nor have the veteran warriors mentioned it.

General Sheridan must have been close to the truth when, in his official report, he referred to the tired condition of Custer's men and their horses and to the frightening conduct of the Indians as being important factors in shattering the courage of the soldiers. Mention has already been made of how those same conditions greatly agitated Reno's men as they left their timber position in the valley.

There are other conditions that contributed to the discouragement of the Custer men. They spent an hour and a half fighting the surrounding Indians, and during this time they could get no more than a bewildering jumble of kaleidoscopic glimpses of their assailants. In his testimony at the Reno trial, Captain Benteen spoke of the constant flittings of hidden warriors around his men on the hilltop during the many hours of their combat. Lieutenant Edgerly testified: "We could not see any Indians. They were behind the points, but there were a great many of them there, and we could just see heads popping up."

It is quite possible that Custer had his men fire volley signals calling Reno and Benteen to come. It is possible that he did this chiefly to bolster up courage that appeared to be waning. It can be argued that, if half of Custer's men had been as courageous as Custer himself and a few others with him, the soldiers could have held the Indians at bay until either Reno and Benteen came to their rescue or darkness brought an end to the fighting. But, since the volleys were fired, and since the discouraged soldiers were hoping the other detachments would come in response, the fact that they did not come at once augmented the discouragement.

Although there may have been only a few soldiers who died during the slow fighting of the pitched battle period, there were undoubtedly wounded soldiers here and there among the various troops. Every wounded and bleeding man would have wanted a drink of water. It is probable that whatever water had been brought in canteens was soon gone. Plenty of good water was available in the Little Bighorn River, which was flowing along the base of the hills, little more than half a mile away. But between the soldiers and the river there were unknown hundreds of Indian warriors hidden in the gullies and the gulches. Custer probably sent Lieutenant Smith's troop down the slope in that direction for the special purpose of gaining access to the river. It is known from the veteran warrior narrators that those segregated soldiers were overwhelmed in a few minutes.

That movement of troops probably raised the hopes of the soldiers. But their mental state must have been worse than ever when the effort failed, and especially when it failed so quickly. Moreover, the main body of soldiers yet along the ridge could see that incident. They could see the horses of Smith's troop crashing among the men and then dashing away from them toward the river. They could see the Indians swarming around those soldiers and rushing toward and among them. Perhaps they saw clearly some suicidal acts. It seems certain that they saw the soldiers being swiftly vanquished and the warriors milling over that ground and surging on toward the battle ridge. All of that tragic sight must have been a heavy additional jolt to the observers who were already in the depths of mental depression. Not only had the attempt to gain access to the water failed, but the men sent to make the effort had perished—or, as was probably imagined, were being prepared for or put to excruciating tortures.

The soldiers along the ridge could not go to the aid of the troop led toward the river by Lieutenants Smith and Sturgis. Just after the lone troop had left the ridge, the Indian activities there increased. Horses were breaking loose everywhere. That feature in the battle's course was the one tremendous finishing blow to whatever hope might have been lingering among the soldiers up to that time.

One can imagine the scene. They were a body of cavalrymen on foot, hundreds of miles from home, in a strange and wild country, and with no signs of Reno or Benteen or any other assistance. All of them were thirsty. Wounded men were begging or crying for water. The Indian war songs and death-wails were swelling louder and louder to a deafening din. Their terrifying facial and bodily paintings were coming more clearly into view as the warriors thronged closer and closer. They were wriggling forward to make coup touches, which were mistaken as efforts to capture alive. Surely, that must have seemed to be the "last-resort" moment—the moment contemplated for application of the dismal precept: "When fighting Indians, keep the last bullet for yourself."

The tales of veteran warriors about apparent fighting among the soldiers themselves may have referred to instances of mutual last-resort pacts—"If the time comes, we will shoot each other"—being put into effect. It is not outside the bounds of probability, however, to think that there actually may have been some fighting among Custer's men. Military law allows any officer to kill at once any soldier under his command who flagrantly disobeys orders in time of battle or who, at such time, exhibits cowardice or abject fear. Perhaps, one or more cases of such execution occurred in the Custer battle. It may be that a despotic killing intended to prevent a general panic stirred up instead a retaliatory movement involving a sufficient number of men to cause a chaos that up until then had been merely threatening.

Extensive theories along this line could be developed. The theories might include such factors as the large number of recruits unaccustomed to military discipline and military law. One can recall Captain Benteen. Although he talked more fully than anyone else at the Reno trial, he probably refrained from telling all that he thought. It seems highly significant that his stated opinion of a panic by Custer's soldiers is coupled with the statement that "many orders might have been given, but few obeyed." It would seem that Godfrey could have said more about the soldier on Reno Hill who refused to go with his comrades for a charge toward the surrounding Indians. Godfrey merely says that after the charge—while the soldier was "crying like a child" and was still hiding in the sheltering pit—"he was shot in the head and killed instantly."

One who commits suicide with a firearm cannot avoid having its muzzle close to his body. If the weapon is directed toward the bare skin of the face or the body, there will probably be around the bullet hole an area scorched by the blaze. If the loading is with black powder, such as was used exclusively at the time of the Custer battle, some grains of the powder usually are imbedded in the skin of the scorched area. The absence or the presence of such a scorched area or powder marks has often been considered as strong evidence in determining whether or not the shooting was at close range, and perhaps a suicidal act. Of course, the test would not be reliable if the bullet had gone through clothing or some similar intervening substance before entering the skin.

Various officers who viewed the dead bodies of Custer and his men have told of examining them for powder marks. According to their accounts, they failed to find any such indications of suicide or of other shooting at very close range. Although their statements have been centered particularly upon the case of General Custer himself, they have been generalized to some extent as applicable to all of the soldiers. The vigorous denials of suicide in Custer's case may have been in reply to a popular story which later became a positive allegation that he actually did commit suicide. Such allegations had no foundation in reality. None of the Indians knew just how he was killed, or at what stage of the battle he fell. Indeed, the Indians did not know until some weeks or months afterwards that Custer had been in the battle. They did not identify any individuals among the white men. They did not differentiate between officers and enlisted men, between soldiers and civilians. They simply knew them as a conglomerate band of white men who had come to fight the Indians.

There were many conditions that rendered the bodies of Custer's soldiers utterly unfitted for a reliable examination for powder marks. Every one of the soldiers was begrimed with powder smoke and dust mixed with perspiration at the moment he died. The Indians stripped all clothing from them. Youths and boys, as well as some of the warriors, went all about the battlefield shooting arrows or bullets at close range into the dead bodies. Most of these bullets must have made powder marks on the naked skin. Bodies were stabbed or slashed in many places. Bodies were dismembered and the parts were scattered indiscriminately. Most of the heads were crushed in by the stone tomahawks of the Sioux or were hacked open by the hatchet tomahawks of the Cheyenne. The devastating mutilations caused further bleeding, and the blood then mixed with the dust that was kicked up by ponies throughout the remainder of that afternoon and much of the following day.

Two days later the bodies were discovered by Lieutenant Bradley and his men. But it was still another day before thorough examination of the field could be made. This was done on June 28 and 29. The bloody, grimy remains had been lying there exposed for three or four days during the hot and humid longest days of the year. They had become swollen, putrid, discolored.

None of the published statements concerning the examination of those dead bodies has contained any reference to their being washed with water as a preparation for examination. The nearest available water was in the Little Bighorn River, half a mile or more from the various parts of the battlefield. It is unlikely that the examiners had any vessels on hand to carry water except the one-quart canteens. A great amount of time and effort would have been required to carry enough water to wash well the more than 200 bodies to be examined. It may be presumed, therefore, that the lack of reference to the use of water for such washing stems from the fact that no water was brought and no washing was done. It may also be presumed that such statements as "We did not see powder marks on any of the bodies" are merely negative statements and are not to be taken as positive declarations that no marks were present. There may have been powder marks hidden under the blood and dirt or mingled with the discolorations. There may have been bullet holes in heads that were later crushed by the stone tomahawks or in chests that were gashed with knives and hacked open with hatchets. All considered, it is not reasonable to pretend that there was any precision in the examination of those remains for powder marks or bullet holes. Even then, however, an absence of powder marks would not disprove mutual killings, as friends or as adversaries.

Officers who examined General Custer's body have said that it was naked, but neither scalped nor otherwise mutilated. They agree in statements that he had only two wounds, one bullet in the head and one in the body—what part of the body is not mentioned. They further agree that there were no powder marks about either of those bullet holes. All of that is believable, since it is probable that the officers made a more careful examination in his case. Yet, a belief in the genuineness of that report is tinctured with a little doubt. The question arises from Lieutenant Bradley's published story in the Helena (Montana) *Herald*, July 25, 1876. Discussing the examination of General Custer's body, Bradley wrote:

Even the wounds that caused his death were scarcely dis-
coverable (though the body was entirely naked), so much so
that when afterwards I asked the gentlemen whom I accompanied whether they had observed his wounds, they
were forced to say they had not.

It appears that the officers who examined the Custer battlefield
smoothed over or suppressed some details about which they had
knowledge, but which they regarded as too shocking to reveal.
The entire situation was a skeleton in the closet of the United
States Army in general, and of the Seventh Cavalry in particular.
From the military point of view, the officers' cover-up and silence
was laudable. But, at times, the silence was broken, revealing a
conspiracy to conceal actual conditions. For example, further
along in Lieutenant Bradley's story in the Helena *Herald* he
wrote:

Probably never did hero who had fallen upon the field of
battle appear so much to have died a natural death. His expression was rather that of a man who had fallen asleep and
enjoyed peaceful dreams, than of one who had met his death
amid such fearful scenes as that field had witnessed, the features being wholly without ghastliness or any impress of fear,
horror, or despair. He had died as he had lived—a hero—and
excited the remark from those who had known him there,
"You could almost imagine him standing before you."

That good-hearted effort to console the grief of mourning
friends overstepped the bounds of common sense. True, there is no
sure ground for positive disbelief of the statements that powder
marks and mutilations were absent in Custer's case, since neither
the veteran warriors nor anybody else except those officers ever
knew of his case in particular. But the sentimental depicting of
his condition as being not in the least gruesome is out of joint with
the natural law. All of the other bodies, whether mutilated or not,
were bloated and discolored, and they were decomposing as a
result of the three or four days of exposure to the hot sunshine
and millions of flies. It seems safe to presume that all of those
natural destructive elements were at work upon General Custer's
body. Even though he was spared from human ravages, it is in-
conceivable that Nature would single him out for pity and refuge
from her ravages.

What prompted the examining officers to think of searching for
powder marks or other indications of suicide? They probably
shared the thoughts expressed by Captain Benteen—that the en-

counter had been "a rout, a panic, until the last man was killed."
The special examination said to have been made of Custer's body
may have been simply to find out what happened in his case.
It may have been regarded as altogether probable that many
others had suicidal marks and that there was no need to examine
them carefully in order to learn what had happened to them. It
appears that Benteen was the Seventh Cavalry officer there who
gained and kept the highest regard of his associates. The fact that
he was the one who broke out in his bold and rugged way to tell
what he thought of the military failure may be connected with
the high regard in which he was held. The lack of statements by
others may indicate that Benteen's associate officers really believed the same as he did. It seems reasonable to assume that
those officers settled upon an opinion that, if any soldier there
"fought to the last cartridge," he used that last cartridge for his
own destruction, or, more likely, he made such use of one of his
cartridges long before the last one was reached.

There is no clue for determining at what point in the battle
Custer himself was killed. His headquarters position at the west
end of the ridge was with the troop of Captain George W. Yates,
the senior subordinate officer with the Custer detachment. Of the
two bullet wounds he is said to have had, one might have been
made by the promiscuous shooting into the bodies after they were
dead. Whenever Custer was killed, he would have been succeeded as commander automatically by Captain Yates. If Yates
had already been killed, the next surviving officer in the line of
seniority would have become commander.

One notable feature on the battlefield points to the probability
that General Custer was killed rather early in the battle or, at
least, that he was not one of the final surviving group. This significant feature consists in the number of officers' bodies found in
the group where he fell. The officers in that spot should have been
General Custer, Adjutant Cooke, Captain Yates and his lieutenant
Reilly, and probably Dr. G. W. Lord, the surgeon. But the bodies
of three other officers were also found in that headquarters group.
One was that of Lieutenant Smith, whose troop had collapsed so
quickly on the lower slope toward the river. He probably made
his own escape and joined the headquarters group. The other two
were Captain Tom Custer and his lieutenant Henry Harrington,
of the C Troop, which had been stationed next at the eastward
from the headquarters troop. The presence of Tom Custer's body
intimates that he was the final commander, after both General
Custer and Captain Yates had been killed. Captain Keogh had

been Tom Custer's senior, but it may be that Keogh also had been killed.

Another theory can be derived, however, from the presence of the bodies of Captain Tom Custer and Lieutenant Harrington in the headquarters group. They may have escaped from the swamping of their troop, just after the swamping of the Keogh troop, as indicated by the Indian stories of the exterminations beginning at the east end of the ridge and moving rapidly to its west end. This presumption seems more probable than that Tom Custer went there for the sole purpose of taking command. He could have taken general command while remaining with his own troop. Moreover, even if he had shifted himself to the original head-quarters position in order to take command there, he would not have taken Lieutenant Harrington with him, since the C Troop would then have been left without any officer. Tom Custer might have gone to take command at some time before the last few minutes of panic, and then Harrington escaped and fled there when the panic set in. Other theories of this sort might be pre-sented, but none of them offers sufficient evidence to determine at what point in the battle General Custer was killed.

General Custer cannot be blamed for the horrifying events of that day. He had with him a large number of undisciplined men, and he encountered various adverse conditions that were unfore-seeable. There is no sufficient reason to suppose that any officer in his place could have done any better than he did. The prime factor in a battle is the capability of the commanding officer. But that officer must have genuine soldiers under him.

The main question in this book has been to determine how the Custer battle was lost. It seems fitting, however, to divert briefly to consider who won the fight. That Indian honor belongs to Lame White Man, the 37-year-old Southern Cheyenne chief. In many previous battles against white men he had learned how to fight them most effectively. When the soldier troop rode down from the ridge, he recognized the opportunity. He rallied the retreat-ing warriors to the terrorizing demonstration that started the paralyzing general chaos among the whole body of soldiers. He mounted his pony and, in plain view, led the warriors in that wrecking onslaught. He took a bold risk and sacrificed himself for the Indian victory.

But now, why was the battle lost? It has been asserted here that Custer was not to blame, that Reno was not at fault, that whiskey did not deliver some disabling stroke, that the guns were neither inferior nor seriously defective, that the ammunition was not exhausted. What, then, was the cause of the cataclysmic downfall?

First, the soldiers had misleading reports from the Indian Office that only small numbers of Indians were absent from the reservations.

Second, the men were undisciplined. A large number of them had never before seen a hostile Indian painted up and had never before heard their harrowing and heart-chilling death-wail shrieks. Specifically, the one man most at fault was the first soldier "gone crazy," as the Indians say, who aimed his gun in the wrong direction and sent a crazy bullet that started an emotional tornado which whirled all of them at flying speed to ruination.

Third, the rock-bottom cause was the unquestioned teaching that the paramount desire of Indians in warfare was to capture enemies, especially white people, for the sole purpose of torturing them. This teaching, which was based on a modicum of truth, was generated by various selfish interests and was fostered into extreme exaggerations in order to create racial hatred that would excuse the greedy encroachments of white men and would justify the killing of an Indian. Every one of Custer's soldiers was saturated with that sort of education. For them, Indians were diabolical. On a critical day and at a critical moment, they became victims of this indoctrination.

It requires but a slight departure from the usual white thought patterns to understand the Indian belief that a divine power intentionally caused that wave of insanity. There is foundation in equity for their notion that an unseen and unheard mystic bolt from the skies killed those white men who were regarded as malicious invaders, or that an invisible wall thrown up about them reflected their evil bullets back upon them as fatal missiles. Such conceptions are in accord with the spiritual doctrine that every wrongful thought or act rebounds to inflict all of its harm upon the initiator.

Maybe, after all, occult influences forced the white man on that day to make payment on an account due. Maybe, after more than 200 years of racial hatred, the Inexorable Law required General Custer and his men to destroy themselves in vicarious blood expiation to the Everywhere Spirit.

BIBLIOGRAPHY

The works listed below are cited in the text by the author. The compilation of a complete bibliography of works on General Custer and the Battle of the Little Bighorn is a monumental task. The Dustin Bibliography, as published in 1953, is an annotated list of 641 items of reference material, although it has been estimated that this number could easily have been tripled if poetry and fiction had been included. This bibliography is found in William A. Graham, *The Custer Myth: A Source Book of Custeriana,* Harrisburg: The Stackpole Co. (1953), which contains a wealth of source material, including many of the items referred to in the text. A more recent bibliography covering Custer's early career as well as the campaign of 1876 is Tal Luther, *Custer High Spots,* Fort Collins, Colorado: The Old Army Press (1972). Edgar Stewart, *Custer's Luck,* Norman: University of Oklahoma Press (1955), is a highly regarded account of the battle and contains a good bibliography of the event. Don Russell, *Custer's List,* Fort Worth: The Amon Carter Museum of Western Art (1969) notes 967 paintings and illustrations of Custer and his last battle; *Custer's Last: Or the Battle of the Little Bighorn in Picturesque Perspective* (1968) by the same author and publisher contains a bibliography of works about the battle and its pictorial representations.

Bourke, John G. *On the Border with Crook.* New York: C. Scribner's Sons, 1891. Reprinted. Columbus, Ohio: Long's College Book Co., 1950.

Bradley, Lieutenant James H. "Journal of Sioux Campaign of 1876." *Montana Historical Society Contributions,* Vol. II, 1896. Reprinted with additional materials. *The March of the Montana Column: A Prelude to the Custer Disaster.* Norman: University of Oklahoma Press, 1961.

Brady, Cyrus Townsend. *Indian Fights and Fighters.* Garden City: Doubleday, 1923.

Brininstool, Earl A. *A Trooper with Custer.* Columbus, Ohio: Hunter-Trader-Trapper, 1925. Revised and expanded edition. *Troopers with Custer: Historic Incidents of the Battle of the Little Big Horn.* New York: Bonanza Books, 1952.

Byrne, P. E. *Soldiers of the Plains.* New York: Minton, Balch & Co., 1926.

Carroll, Matthew. "The Diary of Matthew Carroll for Gibbon's Campaign in 1876." *Montana Historical Society Contributions,* Vol. II, 1896.

Custer, Elizabeth Bacon. *Boots and Saddles: Or, Life in Dakota with General Custer.* New York: Harper & Brothers, 1885. Reprinted with introduction. Norman: University of Oklahoma Press, 1961.

————. *Following the Guidon.* New York: Harper & Brothers, 1890. Reprinted with introduction. Norman: University of Oklahoma Press, 1966.

————. *Tenting on the Plains: Or, General Custer in Kansas and Texas.* New York: C. L. Webster & Co., 1888.

Custer, George Armstrong. "Battling with the Sioux on the Yellowstone." *Galaxy Magazine* XXII (1876).

————. *My Life on the Plains: Or, Personal Experiences with Indians.* New York: Sheldon & Co., 1874. Reprinted with additional chapter and introduction. Norman: University of Oklahoma Press, 1962.

————. "War Memoirs." *Galaxy Magazine* XXII (1876).

Dixon, Dr. Joseph K. *The Vanishing Race: Last Great Indian Council.* Garden City: Doubleday, Page & Co., 1913.

Eastman, Dr. Charles A. "The Story of the Little Big Horn." *Chautauqua Magazine* XXXI (1900).

Finerty, John F. *War-Path and Bivouac: Or, The Conquest of the Sioux.* Chicago: Donohue, Henneberry & Co., 1890. Reprinted with an introduction. Norman: University of Oklahoma Press, 1961.

Godfrey, Edward S. *After the Custer Battle.* Sources of Northwest History, No. 9. Edited by Albert J. Partoll. Missoula: Montana State University.

————. "Battle of the Washita." *Winners* VI (1929).

————. "Custer's Last Battle." *Century Magazine* XLIII (1892). Reprinted with additions by Elizabeth Custer. *General George A. Custer and the Battle of the Little Big Horn.* New York: Century Book Co., 1908. Expanded version reprinted. *Montana Historical Society Contributions,* Vol. IX, 1921.

————. "The Death of General Custer." *Cavalry Journal* XXXVI (1927).

————. *The Field Diary of Lt. Edward Settle Godfrey, Commanding Co. K, 7th Cavalry Regiment under Lt. Colonel George Armstrong Custer in the Sioux Encounter at the Battle of the Little Big Horn.* Portland, Ore: Champoeg Press, 1957.

————. "Some Reminiscences of the Battle of the Washita." *Cavalry Journal,* October, 1928.

Graham, Colonel William A. *The Story of the Little Big Horn: Custer's Last Fight.* New York: The Century Co., 1926. New edition. New York: Bonanza Books, 1959.

Hebard, Grace Raymond, and Brininstool, Earl A. *The Bozeman Trail:*

Historical Accounts of the Blazing of the Overland Routes into the Northwest and the Fights with Red Cloud's Warriors. 2 vols. Cleveland: The Arthur H. Clark Co., 1922.

Kellogg, Mark. "Notes on the Little Big Horn Expedition under General Custer." *Montana Historical Society Collections,* Vol. IX, 1923.

King, Charles. *Campaigning with Crook.* New York: Harper & Brothers, 1890. Reprinted with introduction. Norman: University of Oklahoma Press, 1964.

Libby, Orin Grant, ed. "The Arikara Narrative of the Campaign Against the Hostile Dakotas, 1876." *North Dakota Historical Collections,* Vol. 6, 1920.

Linderman, Frank B. *American: The Life Story of a Great Indian, Plenty-Coups, Chief of the Crows.* New York: John Day Co., 1930.

Lord, John. *Frontier Dust.* Hartford, Conn.: Edwin Valentine Mitchell, 1926.

McLaughlin, James. *My Friend the Indian.* Boston: Houghton Mifflin Co., 1910.

Marquis, Thomas B. *Custer on the Little Bighorn.* Lodi, Calif.: End-Kian Publishing Co., 1969.

———. *Memoirs of a White Crow Indian.* New York: The Century Co., 1928. Reprinted. Lincoln: University of Nebraska Press, 1974.

———. *Wooden Leg: A Warrior Who Fought Custer.* Minneapolis: Midwest Book Co., 1931. Reprinted. Lincoln: University of Nebraska Press, 1962.

Martin, John. "Custer's Last Battle." *Cavalry Journal,* July, 1923.

Reno, Marcus Albert. *The Official Record of a Court of Inquiry Convened by the President of the United States upon the Request of Major Marcus A. Reno, 7th U.S. Cavalry, to Investigate his Conduct at the Battle of the Little Big Horn, June 25-26, 1876.* Pacific Palisades, Calif., 1951. Abstract version by William A. Graham. Harrisburg: Stackpole Co., 1954.

Roosevelt, Theodore. *The Winning of the West.* 6 vols. New York: G. P. Putnam's Sons, 1900.

Schultz, James Willard. *William Jackson, Indian Scout.* Boston: Houghton Mifflin Co., 1926.

Scott, Hugh L. *Some Memories of a Soldier.* New York: The Century Co., 1928.

Standing Bear, Luther. *Land of the Spotted Eagle.* Boston: Houghton Mifflin Co., 1933.

———. *My Indian Boyhood.* Boston: Houghton Mifflin Co., 1928.

———. *My People, the Sioux.* Edited by E. A. Brininstool. Boston: Houghton Mifflin Co., 1931.

Walker, Judson Elliottt. *Campaign of General Custer in the North-West, and the Final Surrender of Sitting Bull.* New York: Jenkins and Thomas, 1881.

INDEX